In Spite of the Headwinds

**My Journey from Waste Picker
to Vice President at a Top-Forty
Fortune 500 Company**

Autobiography of Samuel Moody Santos

WESTBOW
PRESS®
A DIVISION OF THOMAS NELSON
& ZONDERVAN

WestBow Press books may be ordered through booksellers or by contacting:

WestBow Press
A Division of Thomas Nelson & Zondervan
1663 Liberty Drive
Bloomington, IN 47403
www.westbowpress.com
1 (866) 928-1240

ISBN: 978-1-5127-8804-4 (sc)
ISBN: 978-1-5127-8805-1 (hc)
ISBN: 978-1-5127-8803-7 (e)

Library of Congress Control Number: 2017907462

Print information available on the last page.

WestBow Press rev. date: 5/25/2017

Foreword

In Spite of the Headwinds is an absolute read for all Christ-followers. Samuel's commitment to Christ and his sheer determination to overcome every obstacle inspires each of us to reach our God-given potential. This story clearly demonstrates how our God is truly greater than anything we face.

I have the honor of knowing Samuel and his family personally. I can truly attest that this is a man who lives what he believes. He is faithful to his Lord, his wife, his children and grandchildren, and the call God has placed on him. He personifies the call for all believers to live out their faith in every aspect of their lives. Many people try to compartmentalize their faith: families, jobs, hobbies, and then God. Yet Samuel is faithful to God, from his early childhood in poverty to the success of heading up a division of Johnson & Johnson worldwide.

The name Samuel means "answer from God." Just like the last judge of Israel in the Old Testament, whence this name originated, Samuel has stayed true to the Lord despite overwhelming circumstances. From picking up recyclables to the public disgrace of his father's infidelity, Samuel has kept focused on God and stayed true to his calling in life. Where most people settle for little in life, Samuel has felt compelled to fulfill the destiny for which he was named.

As you will read, ever since he was a little boy, Samuel has had a propensity toward the deeper things of God. This foundation of faith has served him well as God has sent him all over the world. Scripture verses fill the pages of this book. Samuel has been grounded in God's

Word and has never stopped growing in his own personal faith journey. He has been faithful to his God, God's Word, and his character.

Through his foundation in God's Word, Samuel stood up to every challenge that came his way. Probably the greatest struggle was standing up to his own father. Instead of projecting onto God the shortcomings of his earthly father, Samuel trusted in God and did not allow the sins of his father to be passed on to him. He even, as a teenager, stood up to his father to protect his mother. Yet he offered his dad grace, and the unfolding story of redemption and reconciliation is one that is an encouragement to all families.

Samuel's story is one of faith. Growing up in extreme poverty in Brazil, Samuel never lost hope in God's provision and love. His story is also one of determination. Although he was hungry and even had to eat rotted food, Samuel was determined to continue on with school. He also maintained the hope that something greater was still to come, and he was determined to achieve it. Samuel's story is also one of incredible integrity. From a young age working at a grocery store, Samuel always did the right thing. This had profound implications when God promoted him to be the head of research and development for Johnson & Johnson–Latin America.

Our lives are all about our priorities. In a microcosm, July 13–23, 1975, defined Samuel's priorities and his destiny. In this short period, Samuel was baptized and accepted his new job with Johnson & Johnson. This set his priorities as Christ first, and then his new career. No matter how successful Samuel became, he always kept Christ first. He became a leader in churches all over the world as J&J sent him to various countries. He prioritized furthering God's kingdom and not just building his own.

We often live life by fear instead of faith. As Samuel reminds us, "Cast all your fears upon God because He cares for you" (1 Peter 5:7). What we see is Samuel moving from a man who, as he writes, was concerned about not doing the wrong things to one learning to do the right things. Samuel has been proactive with his life. He has lived his life for Christ and has influenced the world for the glory of God.

Samuel's story helps us look back and clearly see God's

sovereignty in our own lives as well. Samuel shows us how God puts the right people in our lives at just the right time, like a grocery store manager or a boss at a multinational corporation, to help us overcome challenges, and how he gives us his Holy Spirit to guide us on this journey. My prayer is that God will open the eyes of each of us through Samuel's story to what he has done in our lives in the past and that this will give us confidence about what our God will do in the future.

As Samuel writes, "I kindly suggest that instead of looking at the size of your problem, always look at the size of your God who can solve it for you." Whatever you are facing in your life, never give up, because God is writing a greater story in you. Read Samuel's story and be amazed by a God who can overcome any challenge. And be inspired to be all that God desires for you. God is not finished with your story. Let Samuel encourage and challenge you today, just as he has done for me.

In Christ,

Jeff Simmons
Senior Pastor of Rolling Hills Community Church

I dedicate this book to

My wife, Celia Santos,
my daughter Erika dos Santos,
my daughter Renate Chalk,
my grandson Samuel dos Santos,
my granddaughter, Elizabeth Chalk, and
my grandson Elijah dos Santos.

Johnson & Johnson (J&J), a North American–based multinational company founded in 1886, operates in the industries of pharmaceutical products, medical devices, and consumer products. As the largest health care company in the world, its products are marketed in more than 175 countries. In 2015, its sales exceeded seventy billion dollars.

Acknowledgments

I direct my gratitude to all those who have contributed and continue contributing to the formation of my character. Also to those who, when they first heard my testimonial on how I had overcome adversity, encouraged me to document the facts in either a book or DVD so that my journey could be shared with the largest number of people possible and inspire them to overcome their own challenges.

I am grateful to Mike Wittman, a senior corporate executive who has endorsed this book, and to pastor Jeff Simmons for writing the foreword.

This work would not be an easy read if it were not for the work of my brother Silas J. Santos, whose critique helped me refine my draft into this book.

I thank the people who challenged me during the various phases of my life. You pushed me into bringing out the best of myself, which ultimately culminated in a skill set that led me to senior executive positions.

The greatest thanks goes to the God of my faith, without whom my journey would have been a failure.

Contents

1

Roots

On Wednesday morning, his twenty-eighth birthday, the young Dario dos Santos was filled with excitement. His wife was in labor at the hospital, and he was counting down the minutes until the arrival of his second child. A simple man with little academic background, Dario worked hard at his job of cleaning the streets of the city in which he lived. Their household income also included the little his wife was able to earn with her hand washing of clothes for several families. This couple was known for their intrinsic faith in God, which was even stronger than the love they had for each other.

That Wednesday, as Dario pushed his old bicycle uphill along the steep part of the street, he couldn't help but wonder about the child's sex. Was it going to be another girl, to be company for his firstborn, Sonia? Or would it be a boy, a future preacher? It was winter in that small Brazilian village, but the 82-degree temperature caused the young father to sweat to the point of soaking his dark, straight, well-combed hair. His shirt was sticking to his body, which was tanned by overexposure to the sun. During his lunch break, Dario was headed to the hospital to visit his wife and meet his newborn for the first time.

At the hospital, he heard what was music to his ears: "Your wife is well, and she had a baby boy." Dario became so emotional that he nearly fainted and had to be helped to his seat. His wife, Cecilia, was still sedated, and Dario was told he would not be able to see her or his son until visitation hours the next day.

Amidst the happiness of having a son and the disappointment of having to wait for more than twenty-four hours to be able to meet his own child, he returned to his work. That afternoon, everyone who came near Dario heard him say, "It's a boy." Every boy who passed by, whether going to school or just playing on the streets, was enough to divert the dedicated Dario from whatever he was working on. His head, already heated by the scorching sun, got even hotter when he tried to think which of those boys on the streets his son would look like.

It was a happy day, but it also demanded of him a steep price. The reason he couldn't spend unscheduled visitation with his wife and baby son was that he couldn't afford medical insurance. That afternoon seemed endless as he anxiously looked at his watch every five minutes to check if it was time to leave work and go tell his relatives and friends. Finally, at five o'clock, Dario rushed to spread the news in his neighborhood, especially because most people had bet the baby would be another girl.

As he sped downhill, the wind dried Dario's wet shirt as he pedaled as fast as his old bicycle would go. He went straight to the house of his mother-in-law, Ms. Arminda, to break the news to her. When he got there, he was so emotional that he couldn't speak, and he started sobbing beyond control.

Had it not been for Ms. Arminda's strength and resilience, she would have been in despair, thinking that something bad had happened to her daughter or to the child. "Sit down, brother Dario. I'll get you a glass of water with sugar to calm you down," she said.

Dario sat down on a tree trunk in the shade of a large guava tree and calmed down. A glass of water and sugar had never before been so effective in calming someone. His composure regained, Dario said, "Sister Arminda, Cecilia is well, and she had a baby boy."

Ms. Arminda sighed in relief and said, "Blessed be the name of our Lord Jesus Christ." Although his son's birth was of great importance to Dario, for Ms. Arminda it was just the birth of her twenty-first grandchild. Though he never said so, her calm reaction left Dario a little disappointed. He thought she didn't care, which actually wasn't true. Dario thought he would have received more support had he gone to tell his parents first. However, they lived more than thirty miles away, and he couldn't afford that trip.

Born in 1890, two years after the legal end of slavery in Brazil, my maternal grandmother, Ms. Arminda, had become a widow early in life. Her husband, Mr. Abel, had worked hard and suffered to raise their seven children—Jose, Lucilia, Josefa, Cecilia, Paulina, Joao, and Balbina, all of whom were still under the age of fifteen when he died. Mr. Abel had been a tall, well-built black man always beaming energy and health. But one morning in 1935, while harvesting coffee on the farm where they lived, he was bitten by a snake, and his life was cut short by a good forty years.

Now widowed for twenty-two years and having seen the hardships her own children had faced to earn a living—actually, to survive—Ms. Arminda's thoughts were on the challenges that her newly born grandson would face in life. She ended up having forty-three grandchildren. The old lady was illiterate but blessed with discernment and words of wisdom no doctoral program could provide. A cruel life had been her school. Black, poor, and illiterate, with no professional training, Ms. Arminda was one of those people set for failure in life.

Kicked off the farm because the productive Mr. Abel was no longer with them, my grandmother, whose full name was Arminda Mary of Jesus, had no choice but to gather her children and their belongings and restart life somewhere else, most likely in a semi-slavery job. *A cruel life had been her school.* Now all the children—including my mother, the six-year-old Cecilia—would have to work if they were to survive.

The family traveled more than six hundred miles, from their village of Alem Paraiba to the town of Marilia in the neighboring state. Many people from Alem Paraiba were moving to Marilia, where there were opportunities for whole families to work on the coffee farms.

Those seven children, who had barely recovered from losing their father, soon faced the risk of losing their mother as well. Worn out by the stressful work, and now serving as both father and mother to her children, Ms. Arminda was very ill, and for several days she wouldn't even leave her bed. With no resources and not knowing where to turn for help, she heard about a peasant who worked on the neighboring farm. Once a week, the peasant held evangelistic services on the farm where Ms. Arminda and her children lived.

Someone who heard of Ms. Arminda's illness had invited her to one of these services, claiming she would be healed. She did not have the strength to go to the service, but she agreed the man could come to her shack and pray for her. God answered that man's prayer, and Ms. Arminda decided that she and her children *That faith became central to her life, which was never the same—always moving toward something greater.* would join that group and their denomination, the Assemblies of God. That faith became central to her life, which was never the same—always moving toward something greater.

As time passed, Ms. Arminda's children grew up and got married. Cecilia, the fourth of the seven children, had very high self-esteem. She also had a strong, sometimes aggressive temper and easily lashed out in anger at times. Some of the older women tried to advise her to control her temper, but Cecilia wouldn't listen. They thought she would never marry unless her temper changed.

Enter a young man named Dario. Originally from a different part of the country, Dario in many ways was the opposite of Cecilia. He was white, friendly, calm, and polite. Around 1915, his parents had traveled more than two thousand miles, from Juazeiro do Norte in the northern state of Ceará to the city of Agudos in Sao Paulo. In the northern part of the country, several years of drought had made it difficult to work on a farm because most of the crops were lost. So Dario's family had moved south, where droughts were unheard of.

My grandfather Joaquim with his wife, Olimpia, had eight children: Laura, Virgínia, Maria, Joaquina, Silvano, Dario, Rosalvo, and Maria do Carmo. Olimpia was a tender woman, a lovely person who would do anything possible to help others. I enjoyed every minute I spent with my paternal grandmother, although it probably wasn't more than twenty-four hours altogether.

In their new home, this family of peasants also was evangelized by, and later joined, the Baptist church. My father grew up listening to sermons that helped him to get to know the Bible. He lived a life of hardship, working as a peasant for more than ten hours a day, starting at the young age of seven. At thirteen, he was on his lunch break under the shade of a eucalyptus tree when a bunch of horse hornets attacked him. The lack of immediate treatment almost killed him.

Because it was conveniently located closer than the Baptist church, my father's family joined the Assembly of God where my mother was already a member and active in the church choir. My mother's temper was no issue for my father, so they started dating, became engaged, and in June 1953 got married. Although not the youngest, my mother was the last of her siblings to get married and the only one to marry a white person.

My father quickly became a sought-after preacher and was appointed a presbyter of the church. More than his charismatic eloquence, his faith was impressive. That man could talk with God with unmatched confidence and connection. His good health allowed him to pedal his bicycle for miles to lay hands on people and in the name of Jesus Christ rebuke any illness.

In April 1954, my parents were blessed with their first child. They named her Sonia Arminda dos Santos after her maternal grandmother. For my parents, the duration of breastfeeding functioned as their only birth control method. So shortly after Sonia stopped breastfeeding, my mother was pregnant with her second child.

After my father informed my maternal grandmother of my birth, he thanked her for the glass of sweetened water and prepared to meet his son. He took a shower, shaved, and carefully trimmed his mustache with a shaving blade that he sharpened by rubbing it against the side of his water glass.

He walked and rode his bicycle to the hospital, arriving twelve minutes before visitation time. At the reception desk, my father was so excited that it caused some discomfort in those who were there to visit ill patients. He was celebrating new life, but others around him were visiting people who were fighting for their lives.

That twelve-minute wait seemed to go on forever. To pass time, my father walked up to the reception counter and asked for my mother's room number.

The receptionist answered, "Room? You've got to be kidding me, mister. Your wife and son are in the only ward hall, which is being shared with four other women who had babies yesterday."

As the door finally opened for visitors to go in, my father was in such a hurry that he left his hat back at the reception bench. As he approached my mother, she shouted, "Samuel takes after you, Dario."

Samuel. Yes, this is the name they had agreed to, should I be a boy. It made sense to name me Samuel, which means "answer from God," because I was everything for which they had asked God—a healthy baby and, if possible, a boy. My full name is Samuel Abel dos Santos, which means Answer from God, Breath of Life of the Saints. My parents had agreed that their children would have middle names after our grandparents. Cecilia honored her mother when she named Sonia, and my middle name is Abel, after my maternal grandfather.

Finished with the name conversation, my father grabbed me onto his lap. Mother's wide, black eyes warned him not to bend, shake, or drop the baby. She was so concerned that she later confessed having asked the hospital staff if they had a *fragile* label to wrap around little Samuel.

Not knowing that newborn babies can't yet see clearly, my father winked and smiled at me, expecting a reaction. When I happened to open my eyes, Father started to sob and speak a language that none of the people in that hall could understand. The woman in the bed next to my mother commented that she had been unaware my father was a foreigner and spoke such a different language. She wondered why he was speaking that language with his newborn. My mother explained that he was speaking in tongues, which seemed to further confuse the poor lady.

My father's farewell kiss to his little baby was watered by tears because he was not ashamed of crying in a public place. When he returned me to my crib, at the end of the thirty-minute visitation, Father decided to pray aloud not only for his wife and child, but for all the newborns present in that hall. With a tender touch to his wife's face, he set himself on the hallway leading to the exit. He felt so light and relieved that he seemed to weigh half of what he had come in weighing.

Back in the reception area, Father grabbed the birth certificate registration paperwork and found the hat he had left behind. Then he rode his bicycle to the registrar to finally get the birth certificate for the son whom he believed would eventually replace him in the evangelism pulpits. Without asking my father any questions, the registrar rushed to issue a birth certificate that indicates my skin color as white. After all, the father standing right there in front of the registrar was white, so his son must also be white.

Dario was the only relative to visit Cecilia and Samuel that day. By the time Grandma Arminda and little Sonia arrived, following an hour-long walk, visitation time was over. Grandma Arminda's sixty-six years of age and the toddler she carried had slowed her down too much to get to the hospital on time.

2

Mr. Dario dos Santos's Household

The small and quiet city was provided with medical assistance in the form of an ambulance from the government-funded universal health care, which took mother and baby home two days after his birth.

My father's house was a 200-square-foot makeshift dwelling with a kitchen, a living room, and one bedroom. The bathroom was a hole excavated in the yard. There was no running water, and the well was just about six yards from the septic tank. This was where I would live for my first eleven years. The only bedroom in the house was about eighty square feet that was at that time the sleeping room for father, mother, and two kids.

In that low-income, working-class neighborhood, word of mouth spread fairly quickly, and so everybody knew that Dario Junior had been born. No matter what a boy was named, they tended to call him by his father's name. Some did believe my father would have in me a namesake. A line started to queue outside the house with people who came to see the new arrival. They were all informed that the baby was named Samuel, but the more they looked at me, given my resemblance to my father, the more they had difficulty in admitting that I was not Dario Junior.

Seeing the baby was one thing, but holding me was another because mother wouldn't easily agree to let them. That excessive maternal zeal contributed along the years for my being, among my siblings, perhaps the one closest to my mother. Six weeks after giving birth, my mother, with two children under the age of three, had to work at something to help the household income. The best solution was for her to continue washing clothes at home because that way she could assist the kids, take care of her chores, and do some extra work, since her husband earned only minimum wage.

The modus operandi for the laundry business worked this way: During his return home from work, my father would ride his bicycle by the homes of my mother's laundry customers and pick up their dirty clothes. The next day, he would deliver the washed and ironed clothes to their owners' houses. I think that to this day, we all dream of a good laundry service that picks up and delivers back to our door. On his lunch break, my father would repeat the same routine because he had to do that for eighteen houses. You may wonder at the seemingly insurmountable task of hand washing clothes for eighteen families, especially while having to draw water from a well. It surely does not seem like an appropriate job for a woman just six weeks after delivering a baby.

However, this job did not seem to be an exhausting one for a woman whose education was limited to first grade, and in the absence of her academic attainment she decided that she would not limit the future of her children to minimum wage. Since the birth of Sonia my mother had taken upon herself the commitment to give her best so that all her children could achieve their high goals in life, something she had aspired to herself but never had the opportunity to pursue. To her a child was a gift from God, entrusted by him to her care and responsibility for success. In the tube where she washed all those clothes, sometimes under a sun of 100 degrees Fahrenheit and sometimes working tirelessly from dawn until dusk, she moved in a rhythm that washing machines are still trying to achieve.

On the first Sunday after her six weeks postpartum recovery period, the Santos couple brought the baby Samuel to their church. It was not a special ceremony but a regular Sunday night service, except for the young couple who would fulfill their vows of dedicating their child to the Lord God and promise to raise me according to biblical teachings. For a change, that meeting went over the scheduled time, making it two and a half hours long accompanied by music that rang out from trombones, saxophones, trumpets, and clarinets. It was so loud that I cried my lungs out.

At 9:30 p.m. the church pastor invited my parents for the dedication ceremony, at which point my mother knew how hard it had been to keep the baby looking neat for more than two hours, especially when there were no disposable diapers. Some of the neighbors came to church that day to see the dedication. I was dedicated in about five minutes and everyone was dismissed.

Uncle Silvano, my father's older brother, lived on the same block as my family. By the time I was born, he already had five children, and his neighbor was my maternal grandmother, Arminda. On a daily basis, my grandmother would help my mother by watching Sonia, since the newborn had to have the mother close by to be fed.

My mother's ordinary days now presented extra challenges, such as how to raise two children with all the other tasks she had, such as washing clothes for eighteen families, chores around the house, and hosting the many visitors who would show up unexpectedly for a prayer, words of advice, or just to chat. The positive side of having visitors was that the baby Samuel was given a lot of talcum powder, baby oil, cotton rolls, baby shampoo, and some washable diapers, which saved my mother from having to buy those things.

The couple was slowly adjusting their lives to the new family size. Medical care was always the mother's responsibility, to ensure that her children were properly assisted and that vaccinations were always on schedule. For my mother, having her own mother just around the corner, literally, was a good thing. In addition to her mother helping out with the kids, they started a business of raising pigs together.

This is how this pig-raising business worked: A gentleman who had his pig farm across the street would provide my grandmother with as many baby pigs as she wanted to raise. When the pigs grew to be big and fat, they *Creativity and seizing opportunities were characteristic of my parents.* were slaughtered. The pigs' owner would take half and my mother, who had raised the pigs, kept the other half. The good thing was that the pigsty was on the pig owner's farm, so we did not have to deal with the smell being too close to our door. The pigs were fed with table scraps from the families for whom my mother washed clothes. My grandmother, who lived by herself, would raise about half a dozen pigs at a time. When the time came to slaughter the pigs, she would sell her half to the pig owner and make some money. Creativity and seizing opportunities were characteristic of my parents.

Don't you dare think that my mother changed her business from washing clothes to raising pigs! Rather, she diversified. My father at this time had three jobs: first, the municipal job of cleaning the streets, which sometimes meant excavating ten-foot-deep ditches and trenches with a pickax and shovel; second, delivering laundry; and third, transporting table scraps and excess food for the pigs. With all that work, they still found time to attend all church services. Their attendance at services and their loyalty to the church drew them close to the church pastor. The laundry tub sat underneath a vine of white grapes, and on Christmas Day after the services, the pastor went to my father's house to taste big, white, sweet grapes.

The older I got, the more curious I became. As her domestic laundry business grew beyond previously imagined proportions, my mother used a makeshift, wooden cart to pick up and deliver clothes. My father had become more involved in evangelism, and his lunch break and after-work hours were no longer enough to keep up with the demands of laundry delivery.

While Grandma Arminda watched Sonia, my mother would carry me along on her clothes-delivery trips. I rode with the clothes in the wooden cart while my mother carried another bundle of clothes on her head, supported and balanced on a rag shaped like a doughnut. She transported clothes this way until she could afford a second cart.

The city of Marilia, with forty thousand inhabitants, was not huge compared with other metropolises. Right through the center of the city ran a railroad that carried both passenger and cargo trains. A wooden fence along the road enabled pedestrians to cross the track where permitted and with proper signs in place. One day, my mother had to figure out how to cross the railroad pushing two carts of clean clothes. She walked up to the track and placed my cart between the rails, and then went back about a hundred feet to get the other cart. Suddenly a train traveling at full speed appeared out of nowhere. It had been whistling as it approached us, but my mother had not seen or heard it.

A railroad company employee, who happened also to be a clarinetist in the church orchestra, was working on the rail a few yards from my mother. Seeing the approaching train, he shouted at the top of his lungs, "Sister Cecilia, run! Take the boy off the track, for the train is approaching and it will crush him." My mother rushed to the track and in a split second yanked back the cart, just in time for the train to pass. That near miss stuck with my mother for a long while, as she realized that her little one could have been taken away forever. I think my mother's high blood pressure began on that day.

Twenty-seven months after my birth, my parents' third child came into the world. It was paternal grandfather Joaquim's turn to provide the middle name. Silas Joaquim dos Santos was born in November 1958. Darker than his siblings and chubby, the new kid would stand out. The usual steps were once again followed: postpartum recovery, breastfeeding, and back to work. In the family's war of the sexes, the score now favored the male side: two boys and a girl. That 200-square-foot place where we lived was now the sweet home of five people who were happy, with nothing at all to complain about.

We children loved to go to Grandma Arminda's house because there we could walk in her yard, which was huge compared with others in the neighborhood. We walked among orange trees, banana trees, and lemon trees, and ate the unforgettable green clementines that were sour and difficult to peel. Also my grandmother used to take good care of her livestock in her yard. She had chickens with their chicks and nests, hatching or simply laying eggs to be used as food. Grandma had neither a pension nor any source of retirement income, so fattening the pigs, using her yard for raising livestock, and growing vegetables were important for her. Her yard had the most delicious collard greens in town because no one could cut them as thin as she would. Because there was no paving, sewage, or rainwater drain in the neighborhood, the street became an extension of her garden where she would grow yams, taro, and chayote. My mother used that same street to stretch soaped clothes in the sun before rinsing them.

Since the home of Grandma Arminda had two bedrooms and was right around the corner from ours, Sonia did not seem to mind staying with our grandmother when she was allowed. Not being literate, when Grandma Arminda had to visit her children hundreds of miles away, she would take along a child not yet of school age but old enough to keep her company—usually Sonia.

In January 1963 another boy was born. The middle name rule had to be broken because both grandparents' first names had already been used. So the third boy was named after his father and was called Dario dos Santos Junior. The size of our family increased, along with my parents' discomfort about Sonia not having a sister to keep her company. Another pregnancy was desired, but the break between Silas's birth in 1958 and Dario Junior's birth in 1963 had resulted, in part, from my mother's difficulty in getting pregnant because of polycystic ovaries and uterine fibroids.

They considered adopting a girl to keep Sonia company. Even today I try to understand how a baby could be company for an eleven-year-old pre-teen. Anyway, it happened that a chambermaid from a hotel in town had two daughters, a teenager who also worked as a maid and an eleven-month-old infant. The mother would leave her baby alone all day long, on a queen-size bed behind locked doors in a house where the bedroom, kitchen, and living room were all just one room. A neighbor helped out by giving the baby her formula bottle three times a day and changing her washable cloth diapers when needed.

Any organization responsible for child care or concerned with child endangerment would have taken this infant girl away from her mother and placed her where she could be cared for twenty-four hours a day, seven days a week. The kind neighbor would not always hear the baby cry, or so she said, and this was somewhat traumatic for the little girl. The child's mother, Miss Maria Rocha, voluntarily spread the news in the neighborhood that her eleven-month-old girl was available for adoption. They lived only five blocks from my house. My parents contacted Miss Rocha and all was settled. The little girl, named Vera Lucia Rocha, was adopted by my parents and became their fifth child in January 1965. Now seven people lived squeezed into our 200-square-foot house.

With no birth control plan, my mother became pregnant again. Even though she carried the infant to term, my mother's physical condition and limitations were serious enough that the baby girl, Sarah Olympia, was stillborn in October 1965. The disappointment and great sadness was noticeable in both of my parents, but at no time would they question God or their faith in him because of what had just happened. The adage that time heals all wounds did not apply to my parents. Those two people seemed to know how to do anything except give up on a dream.

Regarding the stillbirth, they used to say that it pleased God to be that way, but that they would try again. And so they did. The sixth pregnancy resulted in a boy, David John, who was born prematurely at only thirty weeks' gestation. After his birth David remained hospitalized for *Those two people seemed to know how to do anything except give up on a dream.* three weeks, but he did not make it, and so my parents again had to deal with the pain of burying a child of their own. My siblings and I were left with the picture of our crying mother, who did not want to see her son go.

That was the last time my mother would get pregnant. She was somewhat embarrassed because among her seven siblings, she was the one with the fewest children.

3

A Challenging Boyhood

Meanwhile, my parents' efforts to get a larger and better house were worth pursuing. Now they could sell the wooden shack where they lived and buy a three-bedroom house with running water and a yard that was large by neighborhood standards.

Life in the couple's home was marked by working together to earn the minimum necessary to live with dignity. They defined dignity, in part, as the practice of an intrinsic belief in the biblical teachings and traditions they received in the evangelical church they attended. From my childhood, I remember going to church at least five times a week. The meetings were long and never lasted less than two hours. For those babies who would go in cloth diapers and plastic pull-up pants, their mothers had the additional challenge of taking care of them. In spite of the loud sounds in the church, at four years old I could not stay awake, so halfway through the services I would fall asleep. As there was a younger brother to take my mother's lap, I was left in the lap of a volunteer who sat next to my mother—either in the orchestra, where she played her mandolin, or in the choir, where she was one of the indispensable sopranos. Nilza Green was most often the volunteer who held me.

Every time we had to go to church, my mother used to call me, saying, "Samuel, come get ready for church." She then poured water from a bucket, gave me a bath, and dressed me in my only church attire, which included vulcanized rubber shoes, short pants, a white shirt, and white socks. After listening dozens of times to her use those same words to call me to get ready for church, out of curiosity I asked my mother, "Why do we go to church?" She replied, "To see Jesus pass by." I was definitely curious, and when we got to church, as long as I was awake, I paid attention to every single move so that I wouldn't miss seeing Jesus passing by. I even had in my mind this image of a tall man with an impeccable white robe, as clean as the clothes my mother washed. I was waiting for the moment he would walk down the long aisle of that church, but that didn't happen. I then assumed Jesus had given up because the service was too long, and that he couldn't wait for his turn because he had to be somewhere else.

Next week, I heard the same call: "Samuel, get ready to go to church!" I then asked again, "Mom, why again do we go to church every day?" In fact it wasn't every day, but it surely seemed like that to me. And she had the same answer: "My son, we go to church to see Jesus pass by." Four years old and a smart-ass, I argued back, "Last week I went to church and saw no Jesus passing by." My mother promptly answered that I had not seen Jesus pass by because I had fallen asleep during the service. Fifty-five years later as I write this book, I vividly remember that answer.

From time to time in the neighborhood, the police showed up and took away young people arrested for theft or drug trafficking. My parents chose wisely by keeping us in church, where we received biblical teaching. That was the best way they knew to train up their children in the way they should grow.

Christmas was the most anticipated season at church because the children, wearing new clothes and shoes, would recite poetry and sing Christmas carols. We also got to watch the sower play, in which two boys with little hoes would rake the flowers thrown on the floor by the girls. Many times I wanted to be one of those boys, but the same boys, who seemed to have a season pass, took those roles every year.

Every child who wanted to be in a play, or those whose parents had decided they would participate, was given a poem to recite in church on Christmas Eve. My mother volunteered us to recite poems, even when we couldn't yet read. She would read them to us at home as many times as necessary so that we could memorize them. After all, forgetting part of the poem on stage was unacceptable and shameful.

Every Christmas, my siblings and I were each given a six-ounce bottle of guarana soda to drink. I recall crying one Christmas while drinking my annual glass of guarana because my father by my side was drinking a glass of water. He had not been able to afford to buy guarana for the whole family. With tears in my eyes, I held my glass up to his mouth and asked him to drink some. I insisted that it tasted good and that I had enough for both of us. So that I would stop crying, he had a sip—and I felt good because I had given my father a Christmas gift.

On Christmas Day, my brother Silas and I would knock on the doors of those families for whom my mother washed clothes. Then we would ask for a holiday season gift, which meant something left over from their Christmas banquets. Gathering a turkey thigh here, and somewhere else a cold bit of lasagna, we would return home to enjoy an otherwise unaffordable Christmas Day lunch. We had not quite figured out that by accepting that food, we were competing with the pigs.

I recall that new shoes and clothes were bought once a year, just before Christmas. Though twenty-seven months in age separated my brother and me, everything was bought the same except in size. The fact is that my parents would buy the best they could afford, even when that meant not buying anything new for themselves. Ten years separated the oldest child from the youngest, and the rule of the house, which applied to all of us—boys and girls—was that if we weren't in school or doing homework, we should be helping out with the many chores to be done.

My parents had almost no time to pay attention to us children because they were working so hard to put bread on the table. In my mother's culture, daughters were kept at home and protected, but boys were supposed to venture outside the house and, if possible, work somewhere else. At age five, my job was to feed the pigs and sell whatever recyclables—paper, glass, and metals—I could pick up on the streets. Every penny counted, to help with the household income.

In picking up recyclables, I was accompanied by a neighbor six years my senior who would guide me on to how to cross the street safely and which recyclables to pick up. This fellow wasn't necessarily helping me, as I learned when I was older, because he picked up the cardboard and best pieces of paper. Then he would direct me to pick up whatever he was not interested in, such as used toilet paper or broken glass, and risk cutting my hand or picking up a disease. Looking back, it is hard for me to believe that someone would abuse a child entrusted to him by the parents. That was my first experience of being cheated by someone who claimed to be my friend. He had even promised my mother to take good care of me while we were together on the streets. I learned that true friendship is measured by actions—not by words.

> *I learned that true friendship is measured by actions—not by words.*

As we were growing up, my brother Silas and I went together to assigned houses to pick up table scraps for feeding the pigs. We would carry a three-gallon container, which was heavy for two children, so we passed a broomstick through the handle to balance the weight. On our way back home, two boys would lean from their windows and spit on us or throw stones at us. They chanted racist slurs and taunted us, making us feel like humiliated second-class citizens. After that happened a few times, we decided to walk on the opposite sidewalk so they wouldn't spit at us. Then the two boys upped the ante by crossing the street and saying the most offensive and humiliating things a child could hear. They even threatened to beat us up if we didn't run.

Carrying that heavy container was already difficult, and running with it was even harder! We ran for several months, however, until the day they shouted from their windows for us to run or otherwise they would beat us up. At that point, to their surprise, we lowered the three-gallon bucket to the ground. Then I took that broomstick in my hand and challenged those two boys to come outside and beat us up. I even said, "If you are men, come. Come to beat us up, and I will crack your heads open with this broomstick." I have to admit, I wet my pants in fear they would come and beat me up anyway, but I couldn't back off. When I saw that they wouldn't come outside, I became even braver and shouted, "The girls are afraid of coming out to fight. Come on! Come on, girls, and beat me up!" That was the last day that those boys provoked us. After that, we passed under their window just waiting and hoping to be provoked. But they didn't— and then the street was indeed a public place.

I wanted so badly for them to come to fight because I did think I should hit them with the broomstick to pay back all the humiliating bullying we had suffered. Still, I was happy that they had reined in their offense. In fact, Silas and I even used to slow our pace to give them a chance to challenge us. The closest we got to a new provocation was the day they were in the window and we stared at them.

"Back?" they asked. "What are you looking at?"

I replied, "Looking at the coward chickens at the window and wondering why they do not provoke us anymore." Upon seeing my boldness, they shut their mouths and closed their window in fear.

While I was looking into making some money by selling recyclables picked out of the garbage, Sonia was old enough to wash the dishes and help with the chores around the house. Meanwhile, my mother continued hand washing all those clothes in the tub. At this time, one of the eighteen families for which my mother did laundry needed a helper for their maid. The family had three children, a dog, and a sizable fenced yard with plants and grass—and it all required care. When combined with all the other chores, the workload had become too much for their maid, so they thought of a young person to work part-time as their maid's helper.

When asked about availability, my mother offered me instead of Sonia, whom she needed to help at home. The offer was accepted, and I must have been the youngest part-time maid in the history of Brazil. I was in second grade, and school ran from eight to eleven o'clock in the morning. Before class, I would swing by my workplace to water the grass, feed the dog, and sweep the paved part of the yard. Since it was offered, I also ate free breakfast at work—as I watched the boys of the house, in their school uniforms spotlessly clean with nary a wrinkle, climb into the van that would take them to their private school. On a full stomach and wearing an equally clean school uniform, though wrinkled from working, I would walk to my public school. This school had excellent teachers who developed their students and provided them with a free midmorning meal.

One day I was really flattered to be invited to the birthday party for the youngest daughter of the couple for whom I worked. I put on the best clothes I had been given for Christmas, and for the first time, I wore a belt. The neighbor next door to the house where I worked was Mr. Campino, a retired Portuguese gentleman who, up to that day, had seemed to be a nice person. Everyone invited got together for the little girl's third birthday party, and that's when I realized that I was at the party to work—not as a guest.

While I was serving appetizers, I offered some to Mr. Campino. He asked to see my belt and then asked me to take it off and let him hold it. I was a trusting nine-year-old, so I let him have it. Then he folded my belt and used it to hit me in the legs with his full strength. It hurt so much, but I was afraid to cry. So I stood there amazed, as I heard him say, "The little slave is so used to being beaten up that he does not even cry anymore."

The people around him laughed and thought it was funny, while I had to face the physical and emotional pain. I walked away thinking that I had never come across such an abusive, racist, and cowardly man. I wish I had had the discernment back then to tell my parents and file a complaint with the police. Instead I went to the kitchen, poured a little bit of alcohol in my hand, and rubbed it over the marks of his beating. Unfortunately Mr. Campino did not live long enough to see what my future held.

> *"The little slave is so used to being beaten up that he does not even cry anymore."*

My parents always made it clear that we were expected to succeed in our studies. Neither of them had gone to school past second grade, and they did not want their children to go through the same hardships in life they had faced because of a lack of education. So this

20

is how they read my report card: An A meant I had done what I was supposed to do, a B meant I would have to try harder next time, and a C meant I would be spanked because I didn't care about success. I confess that I did earn a few Cs, partly because I did not have enough free time to study, since I had to work when I was not in school.

At that time, my parents' evangelical denomination had strict traditions to be followed. For example, watching television and playing soccer—or any sport, for that matter—were considered sins. It was difficult for a child to understand those rules. If I were caught playing soccer, I would be spanked back home with the power cord of an electric iron. So I had to look for opportunities to play sports, such as physical education classes. After all, the church could not interfere or prohibit children from fulfilling the academic curricula. When the P.E. teacher asked us what we wanted to do in class, I had my powwow of soccer fanatics who would all vote in favor of playing soccer.

My only window of opportunity for watching TV was when my mother would go to church for Wednesday choir rehearsal or Friday orchestra rehearsal. I used to go to church with her and wait at the church gate, along with the other boys whose parents were attending those two-hour rehearsals. At least, our parents *thought* we were waiting at the gate. Actually we would walk around the corner to watch TV. With the hot climate and no air-conditioning, people would watch TV with the front doors of their homes open. Because the living rooms were adjacent to the sidewalk, we could either stand or sit on the sidewalk and watch the wrestling show or a soccer match. When they noticed us, the people in their houses were nice to us and made sure not to sit where they would block our view through their front doors.

Between the ages of six and ten, I would follow my parents to church every day except Monday. On Sunday I would go in the morning for Sunday school, in the afternoon for the children's choir practice, and in the evening for the regular church service.

On the way back from Sunday school, we passed the farmers' market, where vendors, mostly farmers themselves, sold their produce, fruits, and vegetables in tents. At the market, we used to buy sardines because that was the only fish we could afford. One Sunday around lunchtime I went to the pharmacy for my mother. The owner of the pharmacy let me know that my hands smelled of fish, and I told him that my father had gone fishing. Then he asked, "And did he catch many fishes?" I replied, "He caught about forty sardines." The man did not say a word, but over time I learned from this episode that I was be a terrible liar. After all, sardines are sea fish, and the sea closest to us was more than three hundred miles away. Since then I have chosen always to speak the truth, even if it could put me at a disadvantage.

In Sunday school, I got my first Bible lessons, which at the time and for that denomination were loaded with a good deal of tradition and dogma. In hindsight I now understand that not every-

Since then I have chosen always to speak the truth, even if it could put me at a disadvantage.

thing was biblical, such as the prohibitions on watching TV, participating in or watching sports, going to the movies, reading cartoons, and men not keeping their hair short. But I learned to filter—or, you could say, to eat the fish and spit out the bones. My love was always for God and Jesus's sacrifice for me, so the traditions of men were secondary and often irrelevant.

On Monday nights, my parents' schedules were open. As there was no rest for the weary, however, my father started leading evangelism services at a coffee bean farm ten miles away. Eight-year-old Samuel went along, on my twelve-inch rim bike with my ukulele tied on the back. In some places, the dirt roads to the farm were covered by an inch or so of sand, which was quite a challenge for me and my toy bike. Thank God that my cousin, who was six feet tall and two hundred pounds of sculpted muscle, also was active in attending those services. I would stretch out my right arm and grab the back of his bicycle, and he would keep on pedaling like nothing had happened—towing me right through the thick sand.

You might be wondering if I really played the ukulele. Well, I was probably the only person on the planet who believed I did. I had taken a few lessons and participated for a few months in the church orchestra, where, in fact, I would just copycat what the young man next to me did on his ukulele.

In one of those evangelistic meetings, my father gave me two minutes of advance notice that I would be the preacher. He told me that he felt led by the Holy Spirit to do so. I was only nine years old and had no theological training, but I knew a bit of the Bible from being a good student in Sunday school. I had also attended Vacation Bible School, conducted in my neighborhood by Magit Hope (Norwegian) and Dorothy Dodd (British), missionaries sent to Brazil from a church based in Chicago. Because of my promptness in answering all the Bible questions they asked, they gave me the nickname Moody, after Dwight L. Moody.

All of a sudden, I was eager to take the podium at that farm's evangelistic service and speak about the sacrificial death of Jesus Christ on the cross so that we all could be saved. My father later told me that I had barely been able to speak. As I went on to describe Jesus's suffering, I cried and sobbed the whole time I was on stage, although I did manage to talk for twenty minutes. Years later, my father told me that several people had received Jesus Christ as their Lord and Savior that night as a result of my sermon. Among those who converted that night was a gentleman who years later would become a deacon of the church and ultimately take over that service.

The evangelistic activities grew greatly under the leadership of my father, who did everything voluntarily and in addition to his many secular activities. Two European missionaries, seeing that my father's efforts translated into solid church growth, approached him and said that their home church back in Europe wanted to equip him with a brand-new, four-wheel-drive Rural Willys SUV to be used in rural evangelism.

My father answered, "Sisters, I cannot drive and cannot afford the gas either. You know, my worn-out bicycle breaks quite often. So you tell your leaders that if they can provide me with a new bicycle for the evangelism, that would be good enough." As much as the European missionaries insisted on giving him the Rural Willys SUV and even offered to pay for gasoline, he insisted that a bicycle was all he needed. Still today I carry this lesson I learned from my father, who selflessly lived to serve God and not to be served. Because he didn't take the missionaries up on their offer, some called him a fool, but I called him a godly man. I used to look up to my father and think that one day I would grow up to be just like him, but that would change.

On his municipal job, my father had now advanced from being a team member to being the team's leader. I was glad because his previous job had demanded a lot of his body—eight hours with a pickax, shovel, or hoe. As a child, I used to look at his work team and think that when I turned eighteen years old, I wouldn't have to look for a job because I could work on my father's team. It was a great joy when his team would work on the streets near our house. I would take him coffee, and I enjoyed getting attention and being spoiled by his teammates, who would give me a piece of candy or a lollipop. I would engage in conversation with the grown-ups, since I always enjoyed talking with pretty much anyone.

An opportunity came up for my brother Silas and me to make a little more money, work fewer hours, and study more. We started selling yucca starch biscuits at the entrance to the city's hospitals during visitation hours. Our father bought the product wholesale and we took care of retailing it. On the way to the hospital, we would encounter a group of boys who apparently wanted to steal our biscuits. I already had experience with a broomstick, so I started to carry one with me when I went to sell biscuits. Unfortunately, the group of boys was large and they were older than Silas and me. So we approached the police officers in the car next to the site and complained about the naughty boys, hoping the police would follow us and reprimand them. To our disappointment, however, the policemen refused to help and instead suggested we take an alternative road. So we began following the alternative street, but it took us twice as long to get to the hospital. Today I would like to see those policemen and *commend* them for being lazy.

Although the biscuit selling was a good business, a better opportunity came up for me during summer vacation to work in a shoe store. The owner took care of the sales, a cobbler handled all repairs, and I helped them both. When school resumed, I did try to continue at the shoe store on a part-time basis. But the job offered no opportunity for growth, I wasn't learning anything in which I was interested, and the long hours began to affect my school activities, so I decided to change jobs.

While working in the shoe shop, I had an experience that was, to say the least, unpleasant. One day the owner was arguing with his wife. As they kept going at each other with strong words, she suddenly threatened separation. All the poor guy could do was to repeat to her some of the offensive things she had said about him, which he claimed were untrue. She swore that she had never said such things, but he claimed that he had a witness. She worked as a broadcaster at one of the city radio stations, so she was well known in town. She called his bluff and asked who his witness was, at which he pointed in my direction. She said, "This stupid black boy does not have a clue what we are talking about." So her husband asked me to repeat what she had said about him. Accustomed to memorizing long poems for Christmas recitals, I think I repeated with 100 percent accuracy everything she had said—to her amazement and despair.

Enraged, she charged toward me with a pair of big sharp scissors used to cut leather. The stupid lady could barely walk on high heels, and she was humiliated running after a physically fit eleven-year-old boy. I ran to the street and away from her, after which she left for her home. Her husband assured me that I didn't need to worry about her because she wouldn't harm me, and he said that I should not talk about that incident to my parents. That's when I thought, *Then why did you not restrain her when she ran after me?* I was surprised that a husband and wife could be so angry with each other, but I would soon learn that is far from uncommon. This remains one of the blind spots of adults. They underestimate the logical intellect and perceptual capacity of children.

This remains one of the blind spots of adults. They underestimate the logical intellect and perceptual capacity of children.

4

The Grocery Store Boy

At eleven years old, I heard about the summer peasants. It was around the time of the peanut harvest, and my town was surrounded by large peanut farms that hired temporary workers from the city specifically to work on the harvest. The truck had wooden boards that were snapped into both sides of the ten-wheeler open trailer. The transportation was unsafe, as I understand safety today, but back then it was what it was. At five in the morning, we set off for an unknown farm to harvest peanuts and be paid according to our individual daily productivity. We had to work from sunrise to sunset, bent forward, either pulling and spreading peanuts to dry or beating a bush to separate the shells from the roots and stems and storing the shells in a fifteen-gallon burlap sack. For an eleven-year-old boy, the wage was really good, and I did it for two summers during school vacation. That made me feel good, as I was able to support my parents in putting bread on the table.

One harvest supervisor was also in charge of paying each person according to his or her productivity. Because I always paid close attention to everything going on around me, I noticed that sometimes at the end of the day, some people who produced less were paid more money than they had earned. Then I found out that the people who received more money than was owed to them were, in fact, related to the supervisor—who arbitrarily measured each one's productivity as it pleased him to do so.

One day during lunchtime, a young man began to wonder what he would do if he was the *cat*, as everyone called the supervisor. With my sarcastic sense of humor, because there were many mice feeding on the drying peanuts spread on the plantation floor, I jokingly commented, "If I were the cat, I'd eat all those mice." Everybody but the supervisor found it funny and laughed a lot. But at the end of the day, the supervi- *Do not make jokes about your boss, at least not to his face or within earshot of anyone who might tattletale.* sor paid me half of what I had earned based on my estimate of productivity. Lesson learned? Do not make jokes about your boss, at least not to his face or within earshot of anyone who might tattletale.

Halfway through the 1969 peanut harvest, my father called me aside and told me that the grocery store where we were customers was willing to hire me at the impressive amount of half of minimum wage, which was the labor law in Brazil for workers younger than sixteen years of age. I tried to argue that the peanut harvest was paying me twice as much. We talked for a while, pondering the pros and cons of both jobs. But my father nailed it when he clarified for me that in the peanut harvest, I had a job for three months with no insurance, warrantee, or benefit. At the grocery store, I would have an income throughout the year. Another benefit to working for the grocery store was that although I was only twelve years old, when I turned sixteen I would get a 50 percent salary increase. We then agreed that I would finish up that harvest season, but at the end of the harvest, I would go to work at the grocery store. I've never been very supportive of working more for less. In this case, however, it was more money per year even though I felt I should maximize the opportunity of getting the most money possible out of the harvesting job.

My mother, who now worked as a maid, a less intense and higher paying job than the hand washing of clothes, had about half of her salary set aside to pay for Sonia to attend an accounting vocational high school. Sonia attended school in the evenings because during the day she did chores, cooked, and watched over our younger siblings when they were not in school.

My mother was a regular customer at Mesbla, a nationally renowned Brazilian department store, where she bought such things
as clothes, appliances, and linens.
Because she was a known face to the
store manager, she approached him to
learn whether they might have a job
for my sister as a salesperson or office
clerk. Without even asking about my
sister's experience or qualifications,
the store manager—point-blank and
rather bluntly—told my mother they
did not employ black people in that store. That hurt my mother pro-
foundly, and she went home humiliated but resolute that she would
never again spend a penny at the Mesbla store chain.

Without even asking for my sister's experience or qualifications, the store manager—point-blank and rather bluntly—told my mother they did not employ black people in that store.

Being discriminated against was not something new or unusual
to my mother. She used to tell us stories of when she was still single
and worked as a maid for a family. At that job, she worked so hard
and sweated so much that her armpits smelled, and her bosses would
demand that she rub creolin into her armpits to kill that odor. A few
times I passed by Mesbla and looked at the staff—and honest to God,
I didn't see anyone more beautiful than my sister. Unfortunately,
being beautiful was not enough. Sonia would have to be white, rather
than mulatto, to be considered for a job in that store.

My mother had always feared that her children would have a
hard time finding decent jobs just because of the color of our skin,
and the incident with the Mesbla store manager just reinforced those
fears. However, she was happy to see what happened to me, her son
Samuel, in late February 1969. That's when I was hired to work at the
grocery store about which my father had told me. For a fortnight, as a
probationary period, they gave me all kinds of activities to do. I must
have done them fairly well because at the end they decided to hire me.

To be officially hired, I would need a health permit (a booklet
including vaccinations, lungs x-ray, and medical clearance to enter
the workforce) from the Health Authority and a labor permit (a multipage document in passport format, where my employment history

would be recorded) from the Labor Department. I would need the health permit first, and then I could apply for the labor permit. In the process of requesting the health permit, I was asked about my age. I was afraid that if I just said twelve, they would think I was too young, so I said I was about to be thirteen. I am sure that for them it meant the same thing, but I thought that maybe thirteen—rather than twelve—would be the number to stick with them. With both permits in hand I went back to work, and on March 11, 1969, I was officially registered as a cleaner.

The grocery store had only seven employees because it was an inherited family business in which two of the owners, Oswaldo and Yvone, worked as well. Of the five clerks, everyone did a little bit of everything, including delivery, sales, cleaning, invoicing, and so on. We had no calculator devices, so I quickly learned to do math in my head. From my first day at work they called me Pelé, after the Brazilian soccer superstar because they saw some physical resemblance, and by that nickname I was known for the six years that I worked there.

The job was full-time, so from sixth grade on, I worked during the day and studied at night. From 8:00 a.m. to 6:00 p.m. I worked at the grocery store, and by 7:10 p.m. I needed to be in the classroom. It was just enough of a break to go home, take a quick shower, eat dinner, and pedal my bicycle to school. With a two-hour lunch break, I took an hour to sleep. I was used to late nights, so after arriving home from school at 11:00 p.m., I would continue studying for another hour or two.

With my guaranteed grocery store wages, I could help my family. My working hours ended at noon on Saturdays, and after that Silas and I would wash cars of people we knew. The geography teacher, Antonio Carlos Telles Franco, used to pay us more than he would pay at the car wash shop.

The grocery store manager was a philanthropist and a board member for a charity organization. Every year that organization would run fund-raising events, including hosting a five-hundred-seat luncheon. The menu featured the typical Brazilian *feijoada*, a stew with black beans, pork, sausage, jerked beef, and ribs, accompanied by white rice and collard greens. Each employee of the grocery store was given a number of tickets to sell. I love feijoada but I couldn't afford to buy it, so I figured out a strategy to get some for free. A traveling salesperson would enter the store and look for the manager or owner. While he was presenting his portfolio to the owner, who was a board member and thus promoting the fund-raiser luncheon, I would interrupt the conversation and offer tickets. The traveling salesman, who obviously lived in another city, wouldn't want to drive the distance just for a Sunday luncheon. Refusing to buy a ticket, however, could jeopardize his opportunity of making the sale to the grocery store manager. So what did those salesmen do? They would buy the ticket, flip it over, and write on the back, "Not for sale. This is a gift for Samuel Santos." My opportunistic strategy never failed. On average I would gain five tickets, enough lunch for my entire family.

The feijoada was simply the best in town. On Saturday, the day before the fund-raising luncheon, since the grocery store closed at noontime, I would volunteer after work to help prepare the feijoada. I was not necessarily a cook, but I could help with cutting up the pig parts, the jerked beef, and the sausage, and sorting the black beans and rice. The chef, who had a restaurant in the city, was second to none, and from him I learned to make a tasty feijoada.

At church, my younger brothers learned to read sheet music and they could each play several instruments, including trumpet, trombone, and saxophone. However, I had no time for learning to play any musical instrument because my full-time job and school left me with absolutely no spare time.

At work I had become well accepted by the customers. Those who discovered that I was studying were amazed, not just by the fact that I was in middle school, but also because they were probably happy to see a black teenager doing well at work and pushing himself through school. Being the favorite of the customers had its pros and cons. The best upside for me was being appreciated by those customers, the vast majority of whom were peasants, simple settlers who worked and lived on farms, and whom I learned to treat with dignity and respect. The main reason they liked me was that when they got home and unpacked their groceries, they found exactly the brands they had ordered. I also reinforced the wrappings, especially for grains that were sold in bulk, so that the packages would not break open while being transported in an open trailer for about twenty miles on a dirt road. Most customers would ask for the best coffee brand by name, and with me that's exactly what they got. I didn't steer them toward the lousy coffee, despite the fact that the manufacturer would give the grocery store staff a free pound each month so that we would push his brand.

I treated customers well because it was my job. But some of them were not used to being treated that way, so they would bring me a token of appreciation, usually live poultry or some other animal. I still remember the rare bird *Aremides Saracura*, chicken, and even a monkey. Benedito, known to us as Honey, was one of my favorite customers. This seventy-year-old black man was widowed, illiterate, toothless, and had no known family members, but he had a contagious laugh and could beam joy to everyone around him. The downside of being the favorite salesclerk was that I worked more than my peers because many customers wanted to be helped exclusively by me.

I was no longer able to attend church on weekdays since it conflicted with school. I finished the eighth grade, which was then called junior high school. At school I enjoyed learning a little bit of English; in fact, I felt that culturally I had progressed with the knowledge acquired in all of my classes. Mathematics was a challenge because we pretty much had to learn by ourselves. Our teacher would give us a two-minute explanation on the blackboard, sit down, and open his medical schoolbooks, which he would then read until the end of that class.

Then I attended a public high school that was farther away from home, and the classes began earlier and finished later in the day than in junior high. My teachers were outstanding, and I seized that opportunity to learn as much as possible. In fact, I admired my teachers so much that I considered becoming a schoolteacher myself.

The Pereira family, who owned the grocery store, decided to diversify and add a supermarket to their business. I worked at the grocery store until Saturday noontime, and then for six hours on Saturday and four hours on Sunday, I worked overtime in the supermarket.

One day when I was in the supermarket warehouse, I walked past the safe and noticed several checks and some cash sitting on top. The total probably greatly exceeded my annual salary. I took everything to the owner's wife, told her what had happened, and handed everything over to her. Her husband, the manager, had just left to make a bank deposit, and he had mistakenly left the checks and cash on top of the safe. I felt pretty good about having a chance to put my principles to the test, and I was sure that what I had done would make my parents proud of me.

Three weeks later I went to the bank to pay a bill for the grocery store. The teller gave me the change and then immediately began helping the next person in line. As usual, I stood there in front of him, checking the change to make sure it was right. I counted it twice, and then a *The sooner you learn the good principles in life, the easier they stick with you.* third time. Since we did not have calculators at the grocery store, I was fast in figuring out that the change I had been given was wrong. He had given me too much change, equivalent to five percent of my monthly salary. I approached the teller, who abruptly told me I had already lost my place in line and that if I needed help again, I should go back to the end of the long line. He complained loudly about what he considered my attempt to jump in front of the line. I swear to God, I wanted to say that he was the one who needed further help, specifically with his math skills—but I didn't. I just told him that I didn't have time to go back to the end of the line, but just wanted to let him know that he had given me too much change—which I wanted to return. That rude teller did not even thank me for saving him from having to pay the difference out of his own pocket. I, on the other hand, left the bank with a sense of accomplishment and an awareness that the sooner you learn the good principles in life, the easier they stick with you.

My parents were my role models for principles of honesty and respect. They also did not measure the effort they spent to support their children in everything that was lawful.

5

My World Fell Apart

In my family we had always had ways of fulfilling our basic needs, such as food, clothes, and a place to live. Everything was simple, but we lived happily. Now, in 1972, in addition to leading the rural evangelism, my father was also the director of the Church Social Assistance program that gathered donations of food and provided help for those going through some tough times to bring bread to their table. When a bad season would cause the settlers to lose their crops and have no harvest, through its social services the church would step in to provide support to those families. As an elder of the church, my father was a role model and admired by the whole congregation.

One day, I was studying in my bedroom when the associate pastor came into our house and held a private conversation with my father. When I asked my mother what was going on, with teary eyes she told me that my father was being excommunicated from the church and was stepping down from all of his church-related responsibilities because he had committed adultery. Three times I asked her the same question because what she said was for me like a big sour pill that was hard to swallow. My father was my role model and I had wanted to follow in his footsteps. I could not comprehend how he had fallen for things so vehemently preached against.

Questions began to arise in my mind. Why did he spank me if he caught me playing soccer, listening to secular songs, or watching a movie? That had been hard for me to understand even when I considered him a saint, and now that I knew he was having a sexual affair with the woman next door, it was beyond comprehension for me. It didn't make any sense at all. How could my father have the guts to punish me when he was doing something worse? How could he demand that I go to church, when in fact, even though he went more often than I did, behind the scenes he was an adulterer?

As a fifteen-year-old son, I wanted to keep an eye on my mother because she was depressed, embarrassed, and humiliated. My mother always had a rejection complex because of the color of her skin. To make things worse, her white husband was having an affair with a white female neighbor. Despite my young age, at that time I became even closer to my mother, and because I was her oldest son, I became her hope for leading the family should my father walk away from his marriage.

Because I was closer to my mother than my siblings, she confided in me details about how she found out about my father cheating on her. One night she woke up and noticed that my father was not in bed. She searched the five rooms of the house, the yard, and the crawl space, but he was nowhere to be found. While she was in the yard, the family dog barked and she asked him where my father was. To her surprise, as though the dog understood what she was asking, he walked to the gate of the fenced yard, entered the neighboring yard, and barked at one of the bedroom windows. Then my mother heard the sound of my father clearing his throat, an unmistakable sound she knew well. When my father returned to bed, though he denied it, my mother knew exactly where he had been.

A few weeks later my father confessed his illicit sexual relationship to my mother, and then to his senior pastor. Day after day, though they still lived under the same roof, my mother couldn't help but feel neglected and forsaken by my father. He had displayed some rage and threatened her, so she took what she believed to be her legal recourse to save her marriage. She went to the police precinct and filed a complaint. The sheriff summoned my father and lectured him on how to raise a family. He went on to tell my father that even with his sheriff's salary, which was several times greater than my father's salary, he still had trouble supporting his own family. Then he questioned how my father hoped to support two families on a wage barely above minimum, but that visit to the sheriff's office did not change my father's drive.

The so-called *husband* of the woman with whom my father was having an affair worked 280 miles away, and he would come and see his family only once a month. To this day I am not sure whether that man was indeed her husband.

One Sunday morning, my brother Dario Junior and I were late in leaving the house for Sunday school. As we were leaving through the front door, we found a bag with fresh tropical fruits, mozzarella cheese knots, a can of guava paste, and bottles of guarana soft drinks. Curious, like ordinary children, we opened the bag to see what we would be eating for lunch and/or dessert upon returning home from Sunday school. While we were going through the bags, my father appeared and yelled at us furiously about being late for church.

Yes, we left for church, but I kept thinking about how delicious that fettuccine was going to be. My little brother mentioned the mozzarella knots a few times on our way to church, as he had long wondered what those would taste like. When we got back home from church and checked what was for lunch, both of us were disappointed to find out that none of the delicacies we had seen in that large bag of farmers' market products were being served. It wasn't hard to figure out that those products had been bought for his mistress and her kids.

This incident hurt my youngest brother and me quite a bit. The man who was doing such wrong things continued to charge the children to do the right things, validating the saying, "Do as I say, not as I do." Of course, part of his salary was now diverted to please his mistress. On the day of my father's birthday, his mistress gave birth to a daughter whom I've never met.

Our yard was long by the standards of the neighborhood and had many trees, such as avocado, jabuticaba, cashew, mango, citron, banana, and sugarcane. We also had a garden where we used to grow garlic, potatoes, onions, and other vegetables. The yard was not that large—just forty-five hundred square feet—but it seemed larger because the house footprint was small. The house sat about eighty feet back from the street. One night, between eleven o'clock and midnight when I got home from school, my mother was at the gate waiting for me. I asked her what had happened because I could see apprehension and fear in her face, but she insisted there was nothing wrong. I wanted to believe her, but her voice gave her away and I could read when things were not right.

I was still struggling to come to terms with how my father could have gone astray. Things he had taught us not to do, he was now taking pride in doing himself. He now kept a five-liter glass container of sugarcane spirits (cachaça) and would drink large glasses of it every day. He became president of the municipal amateur soccer team, but my brother Silas and I were okay with that because we could play soccer without fear of being spanked. My father seemed to be enjoying the freedom to act on some desires that he had contained for a long time. Even not knowing a single word in English, he would sing along with the song "Georgia on My Mind" upon hearing Ray Charles on the radio. He even bought a TV set. For my mother, although TV was against the recommendations and traditions of her denomination, allowing the TV in our house was part of her willingness to permit anything that might help to save her marriage. After all, her husband would be at home watching television instead of going out to God knows where.

For some time, my mother advised him not to drink so much of the sugarcane spirits, but then he would drink even more just to provoke her. A few times I saw him throw on her whatever cachaça was left in his glass, when she would ask him to stop. I would look at all of that and think, *When I get married, I will never treat my wife like this. I will be anything but like my father.*

In conversations with my mother about her abusive husband and the humiliation to which she was frequently submitted, I finally learned what had happened on the night she awaited my return from school at the yard gate. She had been afraid of my father, who had run after her with a knife and tried to kill her. Upon learning that,

I was angry and wanted to file a complaint with the police, but she dissuaded me. Nevertheless, I had to do something to stop the abuse and violence against my mother, who worked so hard for the good of her family.

One day my father opened the refrigerator door to take another glass of sugarcane spirits. My mother again asked him to stop drinking, as he had become an alcoholic. Again, he threw on her half a glass of refrigerator-chilled cachaça, and she was ironing clothes on a summer day, so she shivered as that cold splash hit her warm body. I thought, *That's it!* My mother could be quiet, but I wouldn't take it anymore. I would stand my ground and face the evil. Somebody had to put a stop to this madness.

I told my father that the next time he did that, I would do something about it. I believe my precise words were these: "If you ever splash cachaça on her again, you will have to deal with me. And it won't be pretty, you coward." He said I was just a young naïve boy because I thought I could intimidate him. He then grabbed another shot of that drink, splashed it on my mother, and charged in my direction like a hunter after prey. I called my brother Silas to help, but being only thirteen, he probably feared for his life.

That's when I saw in my father a monster attacking me. I ran a few yards away because I really did not want to hit him. It made him feel pretty good that I was running, so he decided to chase me. Then, to his dismay, I stopped and told him not to come any closer. But he didn't stop, so when he came too close and was about to hit me, I closed my fist and jabbed him once in the face. He fainted right there. My mother came running out and wanted to hit me, but she never did. Instead they called an ambulance that took him to the hospital to be examined by doctors. From that day on, my father never again perpetrated any domestic violence against my mother.

My father's mistress had now moved to another neighborhood, but to provoke and humiliate my mother, he made sure she knew the affair was still on. A few weeks after the woman moved, my father left us and moved in with her. But that did not work out because her teenage boy began threatening to run away. Apparently the other boys at his school and in the neighborhood were mocking him as the boy with two fathers, so my father moved back home with us.

One day, knowing that the husband of that woman was in town, my mother wrote the man a letter telling him everything she knew about the affair. She asked me to deliver it to his hand, and so I did. To my knowledge, nothing happened as a result of that letter, although in hindsight I realize that in an attempt to save her marriage, my mother actually risked being widowed. If the woman was indeed married to the man she claimed was her husband, he could eventually have used violence against my father.

One day, as they were on their way downtown, my mother, totally out of the blue, with her peculiar perception, said to my father, "Dario, I have a feeling you will sell the bicycle. Why?" He denied it, but the same week his bike was sold. With that money, my father ran away from home, leaving no way for us to track him down.

Working as a maid, my mother made only minimum wage, and as a fifteen-year-old I made half of that. My father had been earning one and a half times the minimum wage, so life without his income became difficult. At the drugstore and grocery store, we had been buying on credit and paying at the end of the month. But without my father in the picture, we not only became delinquent but also could not maintain the same standard of living. My thirteen-year-old brother Silas took a job at a paper mill, feeding the cardboard machines by unloading manually one-hundred-pound bundles of recycled paper. With his full-time job, he had to start studying in the evenings, but the half-minimum wage he earned was a big help to our family income.

My father's absence also had a psychological effect on us. My two youngest siblings got their worst grades ever in school; in fact, Vera flunked second grade that same year. We tried to keep my parents' situation private as much as possible, but everyone seemed to have ten confidants, so the whole church knew about it.

Publicly humiliated but refusing to bow my head, I rose up and decided that with or without my father, at my home, we would want for nothing.

Oswaldo Pereira, the managing partner of the grocery store, was a great person and I always felt supported by him. But not knowing what was going on in my life and not intending to shame me, in front of many customers he asked me why my father had not paid the grocery store bill that month. I turned pale as everyone, including my coworkers, stared at me. With teary eyes and looking down to the floor, I—who never talk looking down—said, "I do not know where he is, sir." In front of everyone, I explained what had happened. As though they had something at stake, everyone jumped into the conversation and tried to tell me how to manage my life. The last thing I was interested in was the opinion of some of those people because their own lives were no role model for me. Publicly humiliated but refusing to bow my head, I rose up and decided that with or without my father, at my home we would want for nothing.

6

Time to Grow Up

When I turned sixteen years old, my wages were increased by 50 percent in accordance with the labor laws and I started making three quarters of the minimum wage. This raise allowed me to start paying some past-due bills. My wages, combined with those of my mother and brother, added up to two and a quarter times the minimum wage, which was still short of the three minimum wages we used to make when my father was around. But since we no longer had to cover his expenses, we could make ends meet.

We did try, but not all delinquent bills could be paid off. Bills kept coming, and we committed to working hard to pay them all. Sometimes we had to sacrifice by downgrading on everything we bought, even food. We got a notice from a collection firm that we were about to lose a lot that my father had bought in the next neighborhood over from ours. I went to the developer and explained the situation, and they legally transferred the balance to my name so that I could refinance and pay it off. Many years later I sold that lot to the church and they built a temple there.

Just as we got adjusted to his absence, I was surprised to return home from work one day and find my father sitting on our yard bench and peeling a sugarcane for my two youngest siblings, Dario Junior and Vera. At first, I couldn't believe my eyes, and in all honesty, I had mixed feelings about having him back. As I walked those forty yards from the yard gate to where he sat, in my mind I

41

conjectured that he had come back because, as a loser, he had failed in all attempts to succeed. For fifty days, we hadn't had a clue of his whereabouts. I walked past him and greeted him, asking, "How are you, Father?" One thing I have never been good at is being a hypocrite, so because I did not feel like hugging him or even welcoming him back, I did not do any of that.

As I entered the house, I whispered to my mother and asked her whether he had said anything about where he had been and the reasons for his return. She just said he had been in Sao Paulo, 280 miles away, living with one of his sisters and her family. He had never resigned from his job at city hall, which meant that although he had not shown up to work for nearly two months, he was given his job back.

His actions immediately following his return home indicated that my father was determined to redeem himself out of the mess he had dug himself into, but that posed a challenge far greater than he could have anticipated. One day I went to the pharmacy to pick up some medication for my mother, and the manager told me they could not release the products to me because we had a few months of unpaid bills. He said that my father was surprised and ashamed of me because I had not paid our bills by their due dates, and that we would have to pay off all delinquent bills before they would release anything else to me on store credit.

I was disappointed upon hearing this from the pharmacist. Those bills had accumulated during the time when my father had abandoned his family and wasn't fulfilling his responsibilities as the head of the household, but now he pretended that he was Mr. Perfect and I was a bandit. While he was away, I had worked long hours, including some overtime, to keep the house running, pretty much taking over his responsibilities. So now my father thanked me by accusing me of being irresponsible and not paying the bills? Indeed, he knew we could not have paid the pharmacy bill in full; we could pay only a fraction of the monthly bills, as I had done. The man I had previously looked up to, and whose clone I had dreamed of being, had now become exactly the opposite of what I would like to be—and I had no one to complain to. We do not choose our parents.

It took my family ten months to dig our way out of the debt that we acquired during the fifty days that my father was gone. The fact that we could not count on my father accelerated my aging, so that at the young age of sixteen, I was already thinking like a responsible and mature thirty-year-old man. I kept my faith in God, but I questioned the church, especially for their overly focused approach and demands on traditions rather than on the Bible. The church's social service organization, of which my father used to be the director, never once came to check up on us and ask if we needed help. We could certainly have used their help, but we didn't think we would need to knock on their doors to get it.

The year that I turned sixteen, I started making plans to go to college, even though I was still two years away from finishing high school. I was giving serious consideration to becoming an orthopedic doctor and going to the medical school right there in my hometown. My reason for wanting to stay in town was that my mother would be more comfortable and wouldn't be threatened by my father if he should backslide. My mother always emphasized education as the way out of poverty.

I bought a set of Portuguese-English dictionaries, to study beyond what was taught in my classrooms. To some of my coworkers and classmates, I confided that I wanted to learn as much English as possible because that would open doors overseas—and I

I welcome and trust words of encouragement and totally ignore messages I consider useless.

wanted to work overseas so badly. Some people encouraged me, and others mocked me. Ever since I was a young boy, I have practiced selective listening, meaning that I welcome and trust words of encouragement and totally ignore messages I consider useless.

I have always liked to be challenged, especially when other people have questioned my skills or capabilities. My approach to life has always been that I do not have to prove myself to anyone except myself. It might come across as cocky or

I have always liked to be challenged, especially when other people have questioned my skills or capabilities

43

narcissistic, but my playbook says that if I believe in myself, that's all I need because I know myself better than anyone else does. I answer only to God. So at sixteen years of age, I dove deeper into my studies and achieved even higher grades, which turned out to be my greatest source of encouragement.

Sunday school in my childhood church had been moved to Saturday night, but it was still called Sunday school. Do not ask me why. I was not considered a member of the church because I had not been baptized. Being baptized would have meant giving up things that weren't acceptable to that denomination but that were near and dear to my heart. In my mind, it did not make sense to forbid such things. For example, men in that church were required to have a military-style haircut, but I loved my black power hairdo. I wouldn't have been allowed to wear fashionable bell-bottom pants, and practicing or watching any sports activity was forbidden.

In spite of not being a church member, however, I would show up and show off in *Saturday* school. I had always studied the Bible, so I could answer any Bible questions posed by the teacher, and I secretly always put in the offering the largest amount I could afford. I would study the lesson in great depth before going to Sunday school, knowing that the teacher would test me to the best of his ability. Since I was not considered a Christian role model, he would try to make me feel out of place, but that did not work because I knew the Bible.

The teacher had moved to that denomination from another one, and his teachings emphasized the actual content of the scriptures, rather than the traditions and dogma of that church. Because he had previously been my neighbor, I knew that while he had been a member of his previous denomination, he had played pickup soccer games in the neighborhood. So I questioned his reasoning for trading a contemporary approach for a more strict and conservative one.

Every now and then, my brother and I would try to make sense of what had happened, and we questioned whether my father had ever believed what he had preached. How could he have done something so contrary to all he had claimed that believers should do? We rightly concluded that he *had* believed what he preached, but that somehow he hadn't been watchful and thus had become carried away by lust.

Personally, I think my father always had the desire to rejoin the church and be reconciled to God. Apparently, however, some church members saw in him a pervert, the worst of the outcasts, and someone to whom they didn't want to get any closer. I wonder why those oh-so-perfect church folks didn't have the insight, compassion, or spiritual vision to understand that at that point, my father needed help. He needed an outstretched hand to help him back into the church. Some people would run into him on the streets and turn away their faces or cross to the opposite sidewalk. When he greeted them with the typical greeting of their denomination—"Peace of the Lord!"—he'd receive a cold and dry secular greeting in return. If he'd greet any of them by calling him brother, that would be turned down because he was no longer their Christian brother. The more he was neglected by people who knew him, the more he got involved in some non-Christian practices that were totally averse to what he had preached in the recent past.

On my seventeenth birthday, my father gave me a flashlight. As far as I can recall, that was the only time he gave me a birthday gift. It was not that he did not love me, but since he couldn't afford to give something valuable, he had preferred to not give anything. But now he was making an effort to regain the trust of the whole family—and we wanted to help him, but the emotional wounds were healing slowly. To initially gain someone's trust takes time, but regaining trust takes thrice as long. Sometimes it never fully happens, which is sad because in terms of trust, I believe it is all or nothing. There's no such thing as half trust. Our family's wounds would heal, but the scars would never go away. As my grandmother Arminda used to say, "The one who slaps never feels the pain."

Amid this turmoil and disarray in the family, my maternal grandmother, who was visiting relatives in the city of Campinas, fell ill. The medical prognosis was that her gallbladder complication could eventually take her from us, so we all—including my father—went to visit her. For the first time after his backsliding, Dad would face my mother's relatives. I went with him, giving him some support and encouragement. My grandmother was laid up at Uncle Joao's home, and in groups of two or three, we would go into her bedroom and talk with her.

When my father's turn came, I could feel he was tense, and he went in with my mother. "Peace of the Lord, sister Arminda," he said, to which she replied, "Peace of the Lord, brother Dario." That was the first time in a long time that anyone from the church had returned his greeting as though he was still a brother. My father couldn't control his emotions and cried. He needed forgiveness, but other people had not been willing to forgive him. My grandmother Arminda, however, greeted him responsively and even said, "Brother Dario, go back to Jesus. Look for the church pastor and reconcile to God." She died the following week, and those were her last words to him.

That evening my father and I took the train back to Marilia, my hometown. I could feel that my father was relieved, and he talked about anything but his recent wrongdoings on the entire trip back home. That was when I first told him of my plans to become a medical doctor. I told him how I was doing in school and thanked him for getting me that job at the grocery store. It was a trip that healed many wounds in both of us. My conclusion was that if the religious people who had once communed with my father now despised him, he would rely on whoever would offer him an outstretched hand. As his family, we had to offer that hand. So I told him about my feeling of father-son reconciliation. Upon hearing those words, my father, who barely cried anywhere, started sobbing and cried uncontrollably to the point that I felt I was the father and he the child.

If the religious people who had once communed with my father now despised him, he would rely on whoever would offer him an outstretched hand.

7

Irreversible Decisions

Life was a bumpy road, but we were moving along, and the decisions I had to make regarding a major and college were approaching at high speed. In the grocery store and supermarket where I worked, I got my sister Sonia an accounting clerk job just when she was about to complete Accounting Vocational High School. So now Dario Junior, ten, and Vera, nine, were the only family members not in the workforce.

The worst nightmare for my male classmates who wanted to attend college in another city or state was the risk of having to stay put and defer college by a year because of conscription into the army. Following enlistment, all young men had to go through a basic physical checkup with the army medical doctor (MD). During my medical examination, I told the MD that I had flat feet, for which I wore orthopedic insoles. I listed the many activities from which my orthopedist had recommended me to refrain, and explained that I wasn't fit to join the mandatory training program. The MD listened to everything I had to say, examined my feet, confirmed to me that they were flat, and asked me to go back to the reception area and await his decision. At the reception desk, a gentleman called my name and told me I had been admitted to serve that year.

That decision came to me as a shocking surprise, and I did not like that. Right or wrong, whenever I do not like something, I will find a way of presenting my arguments so as to build a case and change the decision in my favor. When I told the receptionist I wanted to speak with the doctor again, he wanted to know why, so I told him. He was ragged, surly, and in a loud voice that everyone in the reception hall could hear, told me to go away. He said that if I had been judged fit by the doctor, I was going to serve and that was it. I have never been good at being told what to do, so I got right in the receptionist's

Right or wrong, whenever I do not like something, I will find a way of presenting my arguments so as to build a case and change the decision in my favor.

face and told him that I would get my dismissal through other channels—and then I would return and wave it in his face. Obviously I did not know who the receptionist was, but I did notice that in that hall, one could hear a pin drop. Sergio, whom I hadn't seen since we were in first grade, walked out of the hall with me to let me know that I had yelled at the sergeant responsible for army recruiting and training. I said, "Well, thanks. But he yelled first."

Indeed, I left the place in a hurry, knowing that I could be arrested for being contemptuous to authority. Leaving the conscription-recruiting unit, I went straight to my orthopedist's office. I knew the army doctor who had considered me fit to serve was a trainee under my bone doctor, who heard from me that I needed a statement from him that I wasn't fit for conscription. He immediately grabbed a piece of paper, wrote that down, and handed it to me.

Then I went back to the recruiting unit and said that I had a letter, from the army doctor's mentor, to personally hand to him. Upon seeing the statement signed by his boss, the MD gave me another piece of paper that read, "Dismissed for being temporarily unfit to serve." I did not wave my finger in the face of the sergeant, as I had told him I would, but I handed him the dismissal paper with a sarcastic smile on my face.

I was still determined to study medicine, but in the short term there would be more downsides than upsides. I was eighteen years old and my parents counted on my full-time job minimum wage, which I would have to give up if I become a full-time student. Medical school was a long-term educational program with steep tuition, costly books, and other school-related expenses. No matter which way I looked at it, there was no chance I could make medical school work.

Because I liked the English language so much, I then considered becoming an English teacher, thinking that I could later pursue graduate school and become a college professor. That plan would keep me in my hometown, and I could attend the evening program college at the local state university with free tuition and continue to work full-time at the grocery store. Throughout my senior year in high school, we took several simulations of the university admission test, which is similar to the Scholastic Aptitude Test in the United States. In all those simulations, I earned outstanding scores that statistically would place me in one of the top universities. In chemistry, my scores placed me among the top three out of a class with seven hundred students. For all of the top universities, the tests were on the same day, and a student could apply only to one school and had to make that choice before taking the test.

One day I was chatting with a group of classmates about what majors and which universities we were considering. Zeca, the physics teacher, joined in the conversation and asked me what my intended major was. He choked when he heard my intention of pursuing an English major, and he got right in my face with questions and arguments to redirect my thinking. First he asked me why I was considering an English major, and I replied that I liked the English language and had an affinity with it. Then he asked whether I happened to know any teacher who had become fluent in English by going through the program I was considering, and I replied that I did not.

In a somewhat authoritative voice that left me no room for arguing back, Zeca then told me that the records indicated that I used to get better grades in chemistry, physics, and math, and that I should build on that and pursue engineering. To re-

To achieve success, we all need to be humble enough to recognize our limitations and mistakes. We should also be open and appreciative of those who, without any vested interest, provide a valuable point of view.

inforce his point, he added that Brazil was a large and unexplored country with many opportunities for engineering in building roads, bridges, and other infrastructure. He called me *chicken* for wanting to major in English. I guess he wanted to provoke and offend me, so that I would react by considering what—in his opinion—was a better fit.

I thanked him for the feedback, especially since my school didn't have a career counselor. What he said made complete sense to me, and I redirected my efforts toward engineering school. To achieve success, we all need to be humble enough to recognize our limitations and mistakes. We should also be open and appreciative of those who, without any vested interest, provide a valuable point of view. We ultimately own the decision, but nobody knows everything. Everybody can use some help.

Zeca, the physics teacher, had put a bug in my mind. I tried to figure out how to change my plans and pursue admission to a school of engineering, which meant I would be moving away from my hometown because that major was not offered at the local university. My main concern was for my mother, who had not felt threatened or abused by my father for over a year, just because I was around. With the prospect of my moving away, she feared he could backslide. Besides the family unease, I also thought of the effect on my parents of not being able to count on my income anymore. It was much more than many teenagers have to consider when making a decision for college, but I never felt overwhelmed by it.

My plans were then to go to a public school of engineering with free tuition and pursue tutoring of middle and high school students to cover my room and board expenses. Yes, I bought into the idea of being an engineer, but I never considered being a civil engineer. I was set to be a chemical engineer. Now that I had shifted gears to pursue an engineering degree, I looked for a school of engineering that offered evening programs. There were a few, but they were private schools where tuition was a killer. So I would have to figure out a way of getting into a public university and find a part-time job somewhere nearby. Six weeks before the university admission test, the managing partner of the grocery store and supermarket gave me a six-week paid leave, so that I could improve my chances of being admitted to the top school of engineering to which I had applied.

So for those six weeks, for the first time since first grade, I was a full-time student. Three other colleagues and I would study long hours, including nonstop from ten o'clock on Saturday nights until six o'clock on Sunday mornings. I was fully committed to elbowing my way into a top public university. I took the Sao Paulo State University admission test for their full-time engineering program while not quite knowing how everything would be settled in terms of affordability. As I mentioned earlier, admission test simulations indicated that my admission would be a sure thing, and everyone who knew my grades believed they could take my admission for granted.

I traveled some two hundred miles for the admission test and felt relatively calm and confident. The test had no multiple-choice questions. Everything had to be spelled out, so I was in for a long day. Even now I am not sure what happened, but during the test, suddenly I was a nervous wreck. I felt dizzy and got a headache, though I couldn't remember ever before suffering from those ailments. I had a hard time focusing on the questions, and for a while everything was blurred and I could not read anything.

Everyone had expected me to be successful on that admission test, which wouldn't be offered again until a year later. There were ten times more students taking the test than could be admitted. At that time, the requirement stipulated that students would take the test as a qualifying practice. If there were one hundred students to be admitted, then out of the thousands who took the test, only the one hundred students with the highest test scores would get in. Because students from all over the country took the test, results were published in the Sunday newspaper. I browsed the paper a couple of times, but I didn't see my name as one of those few students who had been admitted. My fears were coming to fruition.

I started thinking about why things had gone wrong for

The fact was that I had failed, and I was afraid of facing the people who had expected me to succeed.

me. It seemed to me it was more of a physical than an emotional problem, but apparently one wouldn't commence without the other. At times I thought of church as being a place for illiterate people, such as my parents, but not for me. However, maybe my failure in qualifying for admission to college meant that God was telling me something. Was that because I occasionally had thought of myself as being superior and more intelligent than anyone seeking God or depending on him? The fact was that I had failed, and I was afraid of facing the people who had expected me to succeed.

My sister Sonia, who the previous year had moved with three of her female colleagues to the city of São José dos Campos, called me on the neighbor's landline to hear the results of my college admission test. I told her what had happened, and she then told me about an engineering school near her where the annual admission tests were yet to happen. She told me that although it was a private school, it offered evening engineering programs. Still facing what for me was public shame in Marilia, I decided to travel to São José dos Campos to take the admission test in one of the schools my sister had mentioned.

When I finished the test at the University of Mogi das Cruzes, I told my family members that I would be admitted. I wouldn't have blamed them for questioning my sanity at that point. How could I be so sure, when the results were yet to be published? Furthermore, my admission would not depend solely on how I did on the test. Since the qualified candidates would be admitted to a limited number of seats, the school had to take into consideration how I stacked up against other students who had taken the test. Nevertheless, my confidence that I had done well and would be admitted showed in my beaming smile.

I returned to my hometown and waited a few days for the results in the newspaper that confirmed my admission. Then it was time for enrolling and paying all the fees for that private university. I knew neither the exact amount I was to pay nor how many checks I would have to turn in to the university. So Mr. Oswaldo Pereira, the managing partner of the grocery store, demonstrated his trust in me by signing several blank checks and handing them over to me, so that I could go to the university and take care of enrollment. It was for me a great sign of trust, but without patting myself on the back I have to say that during the six years I worked for him, he saw multiple situations where my honesty, character, and loyalty came through. I made copies of the checks I had issued on his behalf and brought them back to him. Although he had never asked for that, it was a way for him to know exactly how much he had lent to me.

It was early February 1975, and I would have to quit my job at the grocery store. So that I could get severance, the owner fired me, which helped me pay for college for a few months. My mother fully supported my search for a better future, keeping her fears to herself about what her future held with me away from home. Her greatest fear was that my father would backslide, but she was a godly woman and a fighter, willing to face the challenge ahead.

The plan was that I would move to São José dos Campos, where Sonia was already living, and there I'd reside and work. From there, I'd join the many students who took the one-hour bus ride to the university.

8

A Hopeful Move

Feeling protected by my mother's prayer, I left behind my teary-eyed parents and younger siblings, hoping that my decision would result in something good. Holding a one-way ticket, I hopped on a bus and headed to São Paulo (280 miles away), where I would board another bus for the hour-and-a-half ride to São José dos Campos and my new home. All of my personal belongings were packed in a zipped PVC bag that I called my suitcase.

In São José dos Campos, Sonia had arranged for a place for me to stay. I would be joining three roommates, none of whom I knew, and sharing a rented ten-square-foot bedroom and two twin bunk beds. There were six bedrooms in total in the back of the fenced yard of the owner, a widow who lived in the front house with six of her seven children. The walls of the bedrooms were of concrete block with no ceiling and a roof of asbestos tile. In the heat of the 1975 summer, it felt like sleeping in a greenhouse.

The weather, which seemed to be hotter inside the bedroom than outside, was not the only thing that made it hard for me to sleep. My three roommates worked night shifts at the local General Motors plant, and one would come home around 2:30 a.m., followed by the other two around 3:40. Though by no means intentionally, they did make a lot of noise when coming into the bedroom, which was the only space we had. The one bathroom was shared by the twenty-four men living in the six bedrooms. For meals, we would crowd into the kitchen of the owner, but that was never an issue. Because of different work schedules, all twenty-four men were never there for lunch or dinner at the same time. It was also a good thing that the twenty-four of us didn't have to wait in line for the bathroom.

Before leaving my hometown, I had stopped attending church. I liked to play sports, and back in those days my church denomination prohibited any recreational sports activity. When I arrived in São José dos Campos, two of my roommates, who were of the same denomination as my parents back home, invited me to church. I went along and they introduced me to a number of their friends. Soccer was my favorite sport, and the next thing I knew, they invited me to a soccer pickup game. When I asked what the pastor would say about church members playing soccer, they said the pastor's son was on the team. As I explained earlier, the strict traditions had been my hang-up in joining my parents' church denomination, but I started to like this new church. I was confused, but I was also passionate for soccer, so I joined their team and started attending church services.

I moved to the city of São José dos Campos four weeks before classes started and jump-started my job search. In my smaller hometown, most of the jobs were in retail. But São José dos Campos was an industrialized city, so it presented bigger and better opportunities—or so I had thought. Finding a job actually turned out to be quite a challenge, partly because of my work permit. While I was still working in the grocery store, my sister Sonia had advised me that I should have my work permit updated to reflect the job I was doing, rather than keeping the "cleaner" position on it. I had been the cleaner for about six months, but then I became a salesclerk and later a salesperson. Because it was a small business, nobody really cared about updating my work permit. In my brilliance, I had told my sister that I didn't want it changed, because I was going to study engineering. And anyway, I would not be depending on *In hindsight, I wish I had listened to her. But, you know, the younger child likes to pretend he knows better.* the job title on my work permit to help me find a new job. In hindsight, I wish I had listened to her. But, you know, the younger child likes to pretend he knows better.

I was now studying engineering, but in a private school. So I needed to work to pay tuition plus all of my expenses, including transportation to the university, room, and board. The recruitment practice for first screening was to collect the work permits from people showing up at the gate looking for a job. While a job candidate would await a decision, the recruiter would go through the person's work permit to see if there was work experience matching any open position. The few times they called me in, after going over my work permit, was because they needed janitors. Honestly I wouldn't have minded working as a janitor if that would have provided sufficient income to pay my bills while in college because I desperately needed a job. There were many large companies in São José dos Campos, and I believe I knocked on every door looking for a job, but nothing worked out. It reached the point where I walked more than seven miles a day searching for a job. Cutting corners to make it in school until I could find a job, when I was on the streets looking for a job, I would swing by the hospital where my sister worked and she would arrange to give me a hospital meal—you know, the kind they provide to patients. There was no seasoning, not even salt, but I ate it gratefully it every time.

Having the title of cleaner on my work permit was complicating my life and preventing me from getting the job I needed. One day I went back to Embraer, a Brazilian airplane manufacturing company that employed six thousand people at the time. They had a more advanced recruitment system than most employers in town. As part of their scouting, they had candidates fill out a form with details on education and work experience. When the job application form was complete, if the candidate matched requirements for a vacant position, the person would submit to psychometric exams and, pending the results, be directed to interview.

Mr. Fragoso, who was in charge of the warehouse, was supposed to interview me. But when he looked at my scores on the psychometric exam, he freaked out in a positive way and told me that I was overqualified for the job. He wanted someone who would stay on the job for a few years. Based on my scores and pursuit of a college degree, he didn't see me as being a warehouse clerk for the next ten years. He did not let me go, but rather was honest with me and sent me to the IT department, where, according to him, it would make more sense for me to work.

I felt pretty good about my job interview for computer programmer, but my excitement was short lived. They explained to me that the person hired would go through an intensive, six-month, in-house training program. The employee would then work as a programmer on a three-week, rotating shift. The first week would be 7:00 a.m. to 3:00 p.m., then 3:00 to 11:00 p.m., then 11:00 to 7:00 a.m., and the fourth week back to 7:00 a.m. to 3:00 p.m. My ultimate goal, however, was to be an engineer. Working on the rotating programmer schedule would mean dropping out of college, and I wasn't open to that idea, despite the fact that a programmer's salary was just as good as that of an engineer—and I was still a few years away from becoming an engineer. There was no flexibility on their end about putting me on a fixed shift, so I thanked them but declined the offer.

As I unsuccessfully continued my job search, I couldn't help but think that I had made a huge mistake by not accepting the programmer job with Embraer. Then I walked by a temporary jobs agency and saw on their billboard an announcement for temp office clerk jobs. Confidence is something that I have never lacked—in fact, sometimes I think I have too much. After thinking about it for a split second, I decided I could do an office clerk job. I went in, filled out a job application form, and was sent to the neighboring city of Jacarei. In March 1975, I began work as a temporary office clerk at IROCASA (Industrias Reunidas Oca S.A.), with a gross salary amounting to half of the net I needed. I accepted the job because I wanted to have that office clerk job title on my work permit, so that I would be considered for jobs other than janitor. By then, I was using my grocery store severance and withdrawn 401K to help pay my bills.

Early in the morning, I would leave my room and grab my packed lunch, which my landlady would place on a table in the backyard by the kitchen door. My financial situation was a concern to me because my extra cash had been used up. Three months into my undergraduate education, I came to a fork in the road and had to make the toughest decision in my life up to that point. I had to either drop out of college or cut back on daily meals. I thought of my determination to provide a better living for my parents and of the hardships my younger siblings would face should I not succeed and be there to help them when their turn to go to college arrived. With all that in mind, I concluded that I could not give up because my decision would affect more people than just myself. So I cut back to lunch only, and with that I was down to one meal a day.

I recall one evening during coffee break at the university, I was running on an empty stomach and could not afford to buy any food. Classmates around me were eating their juicy hamburgers or barbecued sandwiches, and I would go to the water fountain and drink a couple of glasses of water. On the way home from college, I would stop by the bakery and buy a six-inch loaf of bread. Back in my room, I would break the loaf apart, add a spoonful of sugar, and soak the bread in a one-pint container of water. Then, with a spoon, I would eat my dinner. On a full stomach, I would take a bath and go to sleep. When the water-soaked bread swelled and filled my stomach, that was fine, and I would hope to make it through the night. But sometimes I would wake up and feel like I hadn't eaten dinner, which was true. It's very difficult to fall asleep when you're hungry.

One evening, in the class that followed coffee break, a classmate next to me was eating popcorn with cheese, and I asked him if I could have some. It was a normal thing for guys to ask for a bite of a sandwich, ice cream, or a little bit of whatever a colleague was eating. He promptly filled my hand with popcorn and cheese, never realizing that he had given food to a hungry person who had no money.

I was resolute in pursuing my dream—and if that was the price, I would pay it so that my brothers would not have to travel the same bumpy road.

One Monday during our lunch break at work, I went to the company oven to warm my packed meal, since the company had no cafeteria. When I took my lunch out of the oven and opened it to eat, I noticed that it was the leftover pasta we had been served for lunch in the landlady's kitchen the previous day. I would have been okay with that, but the pasta had gone too long without refrigeration. It smelled rotten and was dangerous to eat. Up to that point, my life had been filled with tough choices, but I had never faced a dilemma like that. I had to choose between eating rotten food or not having anything to eat that day. Fearing for my health but also starving, I decided to eat it anyway. The people around me might have thought I was eating the most delicious pasta in the world because no one could see in my body language what exactly was going on with my lunch. To my happy surprise, I did not get sick.

Through all these challenges, I never let my parents know how hard life was for me. They didn't have the means to help me, and they would have suffered greatly knowing my situation and feeling their hands were tied. I was resolute in pursuing my dream—and if that was the price, I would pay it so that my brothers would not have to travel the same bumpy road. My mother had, in the past, offered to look for a third job to help me attend medical school, but I had dissuaded her by arguing that my teachers believed that, based on my grades, I would do better in engineering. Actually they had said that I would be better off as an engineer than as an English teacher, but I had wanted to preclude my mother from sacrificing for something for which I had an alternate and painless (for her) path.

Now that I no longer had my 401K and severance money to help, on top of my wages, the circle was closing in. I no longer had enough money to pay for school, transportation, room, and board, and I knew I had to try something different to get the financial

I was no different from those people who barely greet God when things are going well. But when things are not going well, they talk to him twenty-four hours a day, seven days a week.

resources that I needed. Back then I was no different from those people who barely greet God when things are going well. But when things are not going well, they talk to him twenty-four hours a day, seven days a week.

9

Finding My Way

I remember the day one of my roommates got home around six o'clock in the morning. I was just about to get out of bed, and he offered me a mug of latte and a grilled cheese sandwich he had grabbed as he passed by the bakery on his way home from work. As I looked at it sitting there on the wardrobe, which was the only un-occupied space in the crowded room, I thought to myself how long I had longed for something like that but couldn't afford to buy it. I thanked him as he left the room and went for his shower, and then I devoured the food like a hungry lion. He was still in the shower when I left for work.

Later that day, it occurred to me that he had offered that sand-wich and latte to me because he had good manners—but surely he had not expected me to take it. That had been his own breakfast after a long night of work and some overtime. He never said anything to me about it later, and I was too embarrassed to even apologize. But I determined that as soon as I could afford what he had given me, I would return the favor—which I did later on multiple occasions.

At work I was always observing my surroundings and trying to learn some behaviors since it was my first time working in an indus-try. I saw a few things that seemed good to learn, but also some that made me sick to my stomach. The owner of IROCASA lived in Rio de Janeiro and was the president of the America Football Club (AFC), a soccer team. When he visited the company, some people in the office would take down the flags and banners of their favorite soccer team and put up even bigger flags of the AFC. Such hypocrisy didn't make sense to me, so I just assumed I would never do something like that.

I felt that life had baffled and buffeted me, leaving me in turmoil. One evening before going to bed, in my despair I thought of praying to my distant African forebears for help. Not having ever done that, I had no clue what it was about, so I lit a candle and knelt. Then I was quiet for a few minutes, waiting for some answers, specifically regarding my financial situation. But that did not work, and my life went from bad to worse.

In my search for ways to move forward, I asked my family to pray for a meeting I would have with the treasurer of the university, though I didn't give them any details. When the university treasurer heard about my situation, despite the window for such requests being closed, I was asked to submit a scholarship application along with a copy of my father's tax return and my work permit. I knew that my father's tax return would show that he had a wife and five children, and that he was exempt from paying income taxes because our family fell below the minimum taxable income bracket. As for me, my work permit would show that I did not make enough money to pay tuition.

In early May 1975, I filed the request and received a three-month full scholarship. With that scholarship, I would not have to pay tuition on the tenth of the month for May, June, and July. That was very helpful, and then I would need a salary high enough to pay all of my expenses, including tuition. But even if that better salary didn't happen in those three months, at least without having to pay tuition, I should be able to set some money aside for the August tuition. My plan, however, did not go beyond wishful thinking.

The IROCASA Company manufactured hardwood luxury furniture for export. In the office where I worked, my supervisor was going on maternity leave and needed an expert in accounting to fill in for her while she was gone. I did not have any accounting background, so to make room for her temporary replacement, I was terminated. Although that job had not paid enough to cover my expenses, it had helped. Now I had no job at all and no financial reserves. With nowhere to turn, I began to connect more actively with God by attending church services and rethinking my whole life.

To communicate with my parents, I'd write them a letter and include a stamped, self-addressed envelope because they could not afford to send me a letter. Since I had left home, without my wage in the household income, they had been counting on every penny.

With nowhere to turn, I began to connect more actively with God by attending church services and rethinking my whole life.

Again I was knocking on every business door in town and looking for a job, though now hoping that my three months of experience as an office clerk would improve my chances. I was behind with my bills, and I had no income and no reserves. More than once, when I was in my room and wondering where else I could try to get a job, I overheard my landlady talk about me, saying, things like, "There is a certain lazy person who neither pays me for the room nor the meals he owes me. Moreover, he sleeps all day instead of finding a job and paying his bills. He even says he studies engineering." That hurt me a lot, and sometimes I cried silently in my room. The truth was that I was not lazy, I was not behind with my bills on purpose, and if I took a nap during the day, it was because I was hungry and had just one meal a day.

One Sunday afternoon, I was on my way to the washroom when I noticed that Carlos, a colleague in the room next to mine, had his door open and appeared somewhat crestfallen. I asked him what was going on and if I could help him with something. I was afraid of disappointing him if he needed to borrow some money from me, but thank God, he didn't ask for that. He said that his mother, who lived in the city of Barra Mansa, about 130 miles away, was ill, and he had just been informed that her clinical situation had worsened. I walked back to my room, grabbed my Bible, and returned to Carlos's room, where I began to read passages in which Jesus Christ was not only healing the sick, but also encouraging his followers to do the same.

I had planned to go to the movie theater that evening with a couple of friends who would pay my ticket, but God had another plan. Upon hearing all my explanations about faith working miracles, Carlos was interested in going to an evangelical church that evening. Again I was faced with a dilemma—going with Carlos to church would fulfill his need, but going to the movies would help me forget about my plight for a few hours at least. But needs trump desires, so I went to church.

On July 13, 1975, Carlos and I, along with our other colleagues who had been planning to go to the movie theater, all went to an evangelical church in São José dos Campos. The church sat three hundred people, who were gathered in the basement because the main sanctuary was still being built. Carlos heard the singing and a sermon on the Christian faith and the purpose of Jesus Christ on earth. At the end of the message, an altar call was made for those who wanted to commit their lives to Jesus Christ. Carlos looked at me and told me he wanted to go to the altar and receive Jesus Christ as his Lord and Savior. I felt excited and encouraged him to do so, but then he turned to me and said he was a little shy about going by himself, so he wanted me to go with him. Because of Carlos, I had already missed the movie, and now I had to answer the altar call as well so that he could stand there for his mother. So we both left our seats and headed to the altar, but I was clear that it was Carlos who had decided to make that commitment. I was just accompanying him.

At the altar we both knelt, along with others who had made that decision, and the pastor led the church in a prayer for everyone who was kneeling at the altar. Following that prayer, the service was concluded, and we headed home along with some people who regularly attended that church, including my sister and the family with whom she lived. As we were walking home, the mother of the women with whom my sister lived, who knew my parents, told me she had thought that when I knelt at the altar, I had made a commitment to follow Jesus Christ. All eyes turned toward me because I was known to have quick and sometimes abrupt answers. This lady was not someone who gave up easily on driving people to commit themselves to be followers of Jesus Christ, so I told her that I had left the altar committed to follow the teachings of Jesus Christ. That was true because I had always believed in Christian teachings, even while I had questions about certain rules and dogmas that had no basis in the Bible.

I never imagined that this news would cause so much celebration. The next day, they called the house where my mother worked as a maid to give her the news. Everybody seemed so thrilled, but I thought it was just a decision I was now aligned to and comfortable in making. Interestingly, to the best of my knowledge, Carlos never made it back for another church service, whereas I—who had just been there to keep him company—never again left the church.

Since I was unemployed and had time on my hands, the next day I sought the church's pastor and informed him of my decision to be baptized. I had been a convert for less than twenty-four hours, which would not give anyone enough time to learn the doctrines of the denomination and everything that my decision entailed, in order for me to be baptized. Nevertheless, Pastor Aristoteles Alencar received me with an open mind, commended me for my decision on the previous night, and asked me a few biblical questions. He told me that I had been an uncommitted Christian for all my life up to that point. But I knew the biblical principles and, to my surprise, he said that my upbringing in the Christian faith made me ready to be baptized on the upcoming Sunday. I received that decision with great joy.

My conversation with the pastor took place on July 14, 1975, and there was a baptism scheduled for Sunday, July 20. Walking back home, I felt relieved, included, and respected as a person. In my arrogance, I had a certain prejudice against pastors, but that man was changing my mind because he was connected to God and an excellent counselor. He had prayed for me, for my decision, and for me to get a job with the salary I needed to continue in college. I confess that upon hearing the prayer he had just made to God on my behalf, I was surprised to see how much he remembered from what I had told him.

As the day of my baptism approached, I remembered that my landlady was a devout Roman Catholic who had shown great concern in taking me in, because according to her, I was a pagan and needed to be baptized. In the practice of the evangelicals, children are dedicated to God as babies. But babies cannot understand a faith commitment, so people are baptized only after reaching an age at which they are capable of making that decision while fully understanding what it entails.

On my way home from the meeting with the pastor, I walked past the temporary work agency from which I had been let go when working at the IROCASA furniture manufacturer. I saw a billboard sign announcing a vacancy for an office clerk. I thought, rethought, gave up, reconsidered, hesitated, remembered the pastor's prayer, and finally decided to cross the street and talk to the recruiter. She treated me like I was the ideal person for the job, which made me feel like someone who had recently been promoted by them rather than laid off.

In hindsight, I think the most common reason for failure is that people wrongly infer that things will not go right— so they don't even try.

That positive reception came as a surprise to me. Since I had been fired by that company a few weeks earlier, I had feared that my records would indicate that I had been an unfit employee. In hindsight, I think the most common reason for failure is that people wrongly infer that things will not go right—so they don't even try. They start off thinking focused on the possibility of failure and are not engaged in preparing and planning for the probability of success.

I came to believe wholly in that promise contained in the Bible: "Draw near to God and He will draw near to you." That seemed to make sense, and my modest knowledge of and relationship with God were my supports to venture into my new job. By then I had done my part to get closer to him, so it was his turn to get closer to my needs. On July 16, 1975, I was interviewed for a temporary office clerk job with Johnson & Johnson. On July 20 I was baptized, and on July 23 I started my new job. In that short time—July 13 to July 23, 1975—my destiny was changed.

10

The Life of a Poor College Student

Someone might call the sequence of events that I lived through a coincidence, and others perhaps think of them as a natural series of episodes in life, but I have no way to identify a sudden and meaningful turnaround except to call it a miracle. Things of which God alone was aware were now being addressed in a neat way. For example, my three-month college scholarship would expire in July, and on August 10, I would have to pay my monthly tuition. If I had been hired as a permanent employee of Johnson & Johnson, rather than working through a temporary service agency, I would have received a monthly paycheck on the last business day of the month. So I would have been paid for one week of work at the end of July, which would have meant that on August 10, I would not have had enough money to pay tuition. Furthermore, I would have faced a 10 percent late payment charge and could not have taken any school tests until my past-due tuition was paid. However, because I was hired as a temporary and my paycheck was received fortnightly, by August 8 I had earned and received enough money to pay my tuition on August 10.

The salary I was offered as a temporary worker at Johnson & Johnson was just enough to pay all of my expenses on their due dates. Remember, I had some big bills to pay, such as room and board, paying for the van that transported us to the college forty miles away, and tuition. Had I not landed that job with that salary exactly when I did, I would have had to drop out of college. I felt like I was living the Lord's Prayer, where Jesus taught his disciples to pray for daily bread rather than for annual or monthly bread. Furthermore, with the money I earned by working some overtime, I would slowly but surely be able to pay off my delinquent bills.

For me, working at Johnson & Johnson also meant going back to three meals a day. Lunch was 80 percent subsidized by the company, and dinner was free because it fell during my overtime period. I was skinny—or whatever you call a person six feet two inches tall and weighing just one hundred and fifty pounds. As I write this book more than forty years later, I can't help but think of the many people who call me skinny today. I now weigh one hundred and eighty pounds, so for those who call me skinny today, I promise I won't show you any skeletal pictures from 1975.

My life was radically changing for the better, but the reality was that my job was temporary, so the fear of returning to where I had just been would haunt me from time to time. To overcome this fear, I learned to lean on Saint Peter's words, "Cast all of your fears upon God, because he cares for you." In the office, I dedicated myself to doing the best job I could. As I enjoyed my new life, once in a while I would catch myself wondering why I had been through so many hardships in the previous months. That made me dedicate myself and push even harder to succeed. Losing that job would have meant not only the end of *my* big dreams, but eventually those of my younger siblings as well.

There were four temporary office clerks working as assistant planners for the manufacturing of production equipment. My supervisor, Juliano Borges, was a former equipment designer who, after leading my work for three months, got to know me better and was willing to help me get a permanent position with Johnson & Johnson. He encouraged me to apply for a vacant position as a draftsman in the machine design department because that would be a better use of my skills as an engineering student and would provide a permanent position with better pay. I agreed, so he offered to introduce me to the machine design supervisor. Following that introduction I was given a test, which was to calculate and draw a toothed gear. Days later I received the information that I had failed the test and they had selected someone else.

I continued working as a temporary assistant planner, and then two weeks later another draftsman position opened up. Mr. Hugo Mohl, a German gentleman, the machine design manager who was known for his cute accent and the tobacco pipe he smoked, called me into his office. Despite the supervisor under him having nixed my previous test, this gentleman offered me the draftsman job without making me take another design test. He had overruled the supervisor's decision that my test was no good. On December 22, 1975, I became a full-time, permanent employee of Johnson & Johnson.

The draftsman salary was almost twice as much as the assistant planner salary, and as a permanent employee of Johnson & Johnson, I would be eligible for a college scholarship after my first work anniversary. When I was hired and learned a little more about design, I recognized that indeed I had failed the admission design test. But I believe that as God had his plans to bless me, it wouldn't be a failed test that would become a barrier. He just equipped me with some capabilities and put me among people who would help me develop and grow professionally. I learned to trust that God was out to bless me.

Every day on my way to work, I thought about what Saint John wrote in the book of Revelation: "What he opens no one can shut, and what he shuts no one can open." I was fully aware that God had opened this job opportunity for me, and that I should then fear him because only God could close this door. Also I trusted that if he eventually were to shut this one, he would certainly open up a better one. I was grateful and beaming contentment for how things were going with my life, which now looked so promising. I was doing well in my good job and my grades in school had improved, but the most meaningful thing was that I had shortened the distance I had previously kept between God and me. The principles my parents had taught me as a child remained strong in me, and drug addiction and licentiousness were never part of my life. However, I still had the idea that living a godly life was achieved by not doing the wrong things. When I learned that living for God also means that I needed to do the right and good things, I then did some course correction and sought his sponsorship throughout whatever life would throw at me.

Two young men, preacher Paulo Oliveira Costa and singer Antonio Carlos de Oliveira (Tony Simeao), from the church in São José dos Campos, were invited to an evangelistic crusade in the city of Marilia. By the intermediation of my sister Sonia, they went to pay my parents a visit and, if I am not mistaken, they lodged at my parents' house. At that time, those young men talked a lot with my father and learned about his spiritual situation. My father was ashamed to return to church, but he found strength through Paulo and Tony, who would be participating in the church service that evening. Encouraged, my father then decided to go to church with them. During the evangelical worship that evening, he felt that for the first time in a long time, he was able to connect with the God of his faith, although some people ignored him in reproach for his recent past and some even looked away from him.

Although my father had behaved badly toward his family, he was by nature a humble and simple man, and he felt strengthened by several people who greeted him with excited joy. At the end of that two-hour service, an altar call was made for anyone who wanted to receive Jesus Christ as their Savior, and also for those who had backslid in the faith and wanted to reconcile with God. When my father raised his hand in the air, as a sign of his decision to reconcile with God, and walked down the aisle to the altar so that he could be prayed over, everyone who knew him cried jubilantly. The news of the week was that, "Dario dos Santos came back to Jesus." For my mother, it was a day of victory and answered prayers, as my father was determined to regain his Christian commitments.

Christmas 1975 was the happiest I had ever had in my life. By bus I went to Marilia to spend the holidays with my parents and siblings. None of them knew of the hardships I had been through, but thank God those were behind me. My accountabilities and responsibilities had increased at work, and I welcomed every challenge. Things were going well at work and in church. Though I never considered myself anything but an ordinary person, some people thought of me as a prominent young man. Again I was attending Sunday school, and because of my questions, the teacher had to be well prepared for the lesson. I began to have money to buy clothes, but clothes off the shelf wouldn't fit me. Dress shirt sleeves were too short and the circumference around the chest too wide. Pants were too short and too large in the waist. My only option was to order tailor-made clothes, and because I always valued a good-looking presentation because of my concerns about personal image and general public acceptance, now I had the opportunity to dress like I had always dreamed of because I could afford it.

Until then, I had flirted somewhat and I liked to chat with girls, but I had not dated. Can you imagine if I had started dating and had no money to pay for the bus to go to the girl's house? That would have been embarrassing, so I had spared myself that discomfort.

Endre, a Hungarian raised in Brazil, was a machine designer and coworker of mine who liked nicknaming everyone. A five foot, five inch tall mulatto colleague was dubbed Little Brown, and for being nine inches taller, I was dubbed Big Brown. I did not mind nicknames; I had been called by nicknames all my life and I had several of them. At home and within my extended family, which includes dozens of cousins, I was called Moody. Everyone at the grocery store knew me as Pelé, and at school they called me Tony because my black power hairdo and physical complexion reminded them of the Brazilian singer Tony Tornado. Now, at Johnson & Johnson, I was Big Brown. Later in my life I even added a nickname to my official name.

11

Rising to the Occasion

My ordinary workday would run from 8:00 a.m. to 5:00 p.m., with one additional hour of overtime. When working overtime, I would get free dinner, and right after dinner I'd walk to the van stop to head to my engineering classes. On the one-hour van ride I would take a nap. Finally I was able to attend class with a full stomach, and I was no longer haunted by concerns about whether next month I would still be studying or I would have dropped out of college for lack of financial resources.

In the machine design department, we developed concepts and designed equipment that would be manufactured by the company for its production lines. Importing equipment was cost prohibitive; the combination of the exchange rate and import duties would have a high landed cost that would be too much depreciation in the final product cost to consumers. Therefore the business of building production machines started to grow. Some machines were manufactured for the Brazil business and some for export.

As a draftsman working under a designer's direction, my job was to design parts for manufacturing. It was rewarding to work with a cohesive and respectful staff. Though based in Brazil, I could experience a little bit of international business. In addition to dealing with internationals who came to Brazil to accept machines built for them, I worked with a planning manager from Mongolia and his boss, the director of engineering, from Switzerland. The machine design manager who hired me was from Germany. Whenever I could, I used the opportunities I had with each of them to learn about their home countries, their moves to Brazil, and their families and cultures. I felt I was getting to know parts of the world without leaving Brazil.

The opportunity to study engineering while working in a related field was a great benefit to me. At work, I could directly apply what I was learning in school, which resulted in professional advancement. I had a good relationship with the manager who had hired me, but he left the company not long after my admission to the machine design department. Until a new manager was hired, our acting manager was the supervisor who had not wanted to hire me as a draftsman. I thought he might question my skills or even fire me, but by the time the manager left, I was already a good draftsman. So as far as the admission test was concerned, I was off the hook. But above all, I trusted that only things allowed by God would happen to me. Knowing that God was in control, I really did not have much to worry about, but felt rather encouraged to pursue professional growth.

Some public recognition and appreciation would occur here and there. It is always nice to receive compliments, especially when we need reinforcement at the beginning of a career. One day, Carlos Cassal, a group leader in the planning department, called me into his office for a quick chat. He wanted me to know that the vacant senior supervisor position had been narrowed down to two candidates, himself and Juliano. And because I had been performing so well and delivering good results in planning, after being hired and mentored by Juliano, the job had gone to Juliano. I confess that I did not know if I should receive those remarks as a compliment or a complaint, so I apologized to Mr. Cassal for unintentionally influencing a decision that had not gone as he had hoped. I also told him that I was just doing my job and trying my best to exceed the expectations set for me. Then I could not help but think that among the four temporary employees, I had been strong enough to be the determining factor on who would be promoted to senior supervisor.

At church I was appointed Sunday

If you want something done, ask a busy person to do it.

73

school teacher and youth leader with the Assembly of God in São José dos Campos, an extension of the parish church downtown. To meet expectations, I had to study the material to teach every Sunday and also prepare and lead all youth group activities. It is true that I was working full-time with J&J and studying in the evening, with virtually no extra time to take over these church activities. But as the saying goes, "If you want something done, ask a busy person to do it." So I was busy, but the activities I had taken over were refining my skills and helping build some new ones. The prophet Isaiah said, "God gives strength to the weary and increases the power of the weak" (Isaiah 40:29).

Things continued to go well and I began to reflect much on the writings of Saint Luke: "Give, and it will be given to you. A good measure, pressed down, shaken together and running over, will be poured into your lap. For with the measure you use, it will be measured to you" (Luke 6:38). I didn't have much to give, but the most important thing was to practice the faith. With the same rule that I use to measure others, God measures me too. As I practiced this principle, the youth group grew and was active. I understood Luke's message—that my role was not to repudiate people, but to include them.

In May 1976, our minister and church leader, Rafael Cabral, invited many in the church to a birthday party for his daughter Elaine, who was turning three years old. At the party there were many young people, and we were all talking about a little bit of everything. In the absence of other entertainment, we began playing a game of staring at each other without blinking. A boy and a girl from the youth group would pair up and stare at each other. Whoever blinked first would lose the game. In one rotation, I found myself staring at the sister of my youth group's right-hand man. She was from the same denomination, but she attended a church on the other side of the city. Neither of us blinked for a couple of minutes, which seemed like hours. My mind was fixed on admiring her beauty, and blinking was the last thing going through my mind.

Seeing that neither of us would yield, I intentionally winked at her to end the game, just as they were calling everyone to join in singing "Happy Birthday" and cutting the cake. When I winked, she winked back. There was a hidden message in my winking—and in the wink I got in return, as well. You know when you're driving and you flash your lights at an approaching vehicle, and that driver flashes his lights back at you? It meant something like that. *Thank you. Message received and understood.* We continued enjoying the party, but my eyes now were following her wherever she went.

It was raining at 6:00 p.m. when she had to leave, and her bus stop was three blocks away. Being a gentleman but with a vested interest, I offered to walk her to the bus stop because I had an umbrella to protect her from the rain. We had barely left the party when she said to me that my girlfriend wouldn't like the fact that I was taking her to the bus stop. I let her know that I had no girlfriend, and indeed I didn't. After we made it to the bus stop, though I wanted it to be late by an hour or so, the bus came within ten minutes and she was gone.

During that week I kept thinking about that girl named Celia, and I wanted to ask her out. I was eager for the weekend when I would see Ildefonse, her brother, in church because I wanted to ask him if she mentioned my name to him after our walk to the bus stop. I did not know that he had already interviewed her and asked what she and I had talked about during our three-block walk after the birthday party. He wanted to know if we were dating because he was some sort of a matchmaker.

The long-awaited weekend finally arrived, and Celia's brother wasted no time in asking me whether I was interested in dating his sister. He organized a second meeting between Celia and me, at which time I thought it would be better for me to ask her before somebody else did. So point-blank I asked her if she wanted to date me, and she replied that I would have to ask her father first. I joked that I was not interested in dating her father, so I didn't know why I would have to ask him.

Anyway, as a man in love, I would have gone the extra mile—and the *next* extra mile—for that girl. So I asked her to schedule time for me to speak with her father, since that was his requirement. First, of course, I confirmed with her that she would be okay with me talking with him. The last thing I wanted was for her father to nod—and then for Celia to nix it.

On June 6, 1976, I went to Celia's house and had lunch with her family, and then came the time for my conversation with her father. He had the most restrictive rules I had ever seen and zero tolerance for deviations. We had just started the conversation when I noticed he was somewhat nervous. Apparently he didn't quite know where to start without messing up his daughter's plan. I figured his hesitation was my opportunity to get the upper hand in the conversation. So I boldly said, "You know, sir, we both are first timers. You've never had anyone come and ask to date your daughter, and I've never spoken with any father about dating his daughter. So we're equally inexperienced, which is probably why your voice is somewhat trembling, but let's be calm and have the conversation."

Up to that point he had said only a few words, mostly about the rules by which I would have to fully abide—or give up the idea of dating Celia. But after my remarks, he noticed that the teenager talking with him seemed mature for his age, so he jumped to the question of when I was going to get married. I told him that I was not proposing to marry his daughter, but rather to date her, but he didn't welcome that thought. At the age of nineteen, he had married an eighteen-year-old, so he most certainly believed I had in mind getting married in a few months. I told him that I would consider getting married only after I completed engineering school. I was hoping he would accept that somewhat vague answer, but he did not fall for it. He then asked me when that would happen, and upon hearing that graduation was two and a half years away, he shouted, "Oh, man, that is too far out." He thought two and a half years was

a long time, but I was comfortable in the conversation and felt we were on equal footing, so I presented my reasoning. In the end, I was cleared to *marry* his daughter because he refused to

When I'm at a disadvantage in any conversation or negotiation, I try to eliminate the upper hand. Or, if at all possible, I try to get hold of the upper hand myself.

give me permission to *date* her. And after that, he would never introduce me as his daughter's boyfriend, but rather as her fiancé—even though I had not proposed to her.

This lesson has always been useful to me: When I'm at a disadvantage in any conversation or negotiation, I try to eliminate the upper hand. Or, if at all possible, I try to get hold of the upper hand myself. I always try to position myself as the person in control, even though deep inside I may not feel that way. My conversation with Celia's father seemed to last an eternity as I carefully listened to his rules for dating his daughter, most of which made no sense to me. Celia's father was an excellent person, a role model for honesty and decency. But at that time, he would thoroughly follow whatever traditions and rules were taught at his church, without questioning anything, because that was the absolute truth for him. One of his non-negotiable rules was that I was allowed to go out with Celia only if accompanied by one of her six younger siblings. So we started dating and I felt like the happiest young man on earth. Finances, family, and faith were all settling in gracefully.

My father's ministry had been restored, and he had resumed the evangelism activities in the rural areas of his town. He was again instrumental through Jesus Christ in leading people to God, and again through his prayers no few miracles, such as divine healing, were happening. I knew God could use his faith because I had seen God heal a deaf teenager instantly after my father's prayer. Though living far apart, my father and I became great friends and confidants of each other. He had nothing but praise for my girlfriend, Celia, and he was happy for me that I had met her. On my shoulder, my father smiled or cried, but we were always at peace and well.

Unlike the tough previous year, 1976 was off to a good start, and God was on my side. How did I know this? At the final exam for structural calculus, we were given just one problem to solve. But I couldn't figure out how or where to start, so it looked like I would have to return the test blank and get an F grade. Then it started raining cats and dogs, and amidst the thunder and lightning, the lights went off. I asked the assistant professor, who was standing right by me, what would happen, and he said the exam would be canceled and rescheduled. So I borrowed a lighter from a colleague and showed my dilemma to the assistant professor. Because he assumed the test would be canceled, he explained to me how to solve the problem. But as soon as he finished explaining it to me, the lights came back on and the professor, his boss, shouted to the one hundred students taking the test that they could proceed and finish the test.

The assistant later assessed the exam and rated the answers from zero to ten, and he gave me a 9.5. To this day I wonder why he didn't give me a ten. Anyway, that situation could have turned out much worse, if the lights had not gone off just long enough for me to get the answer. Again, you could call it coincidence, but the fact is that things like this have marked my whole life in many different circumstances. So I have every reason to believe they were always part of a greater plan designed by the God of love and mercy.

12

Seizing the Opportunities

After my first service anniversary as a full-time employee of Johnson & Johnson, I became eligible for a college scholarship. I was about to start my junior year, having concluded the overall engineering fundamentals. At that point I needed to choose one of these engineering fields: civil, electronic, electrical, chemical, or mechanical. Back then, one of the company's scholarship criteria was that the declared major had to be applicable to the department in which the employee was working. Because I already had experience and a reasonable understanding of equipment design, I thought I would have a more well-rounded profile, and thus be more competitive in the workforce, if I could combine that with my academic strength in chemistry by pursuing chemical engineering. So I submitted my scholarship application form for chemical engineering, and then the head of the machine design department needed to rate its applicability to that department. If rated at less than 50 percent, the application would be rejected.

In the absence of an engineer to manage the department, my submission was routed through the supervisor—the same man who had not wanted to hire me, and who was now temporarily filling the manager position. He had advanced to equipment design supervisor by being a good mechanic who had attended a six-month vocational high school training in equipment design. We got along well, but no matter how hard I tried to convince him that chemical engineering was applicable to equipment design, he would not buy into it.

Because he did not understand engineering, he rated chemical engineering's applicability to equipment design at zero. He told me that my intended major was applicable to the J&J Research & Product Development Center, but not to machine design. I tried to explain that he was describing chemistry—not chemical engineering, and that the major I wanted would be an asset to his department. But no matter how hard I tried to explain it, his mind was made up. He even accused me of trying to deceive him with my description of chemical engineering.

I needed that scholarship so badly that I tore up that form and filled out another one, changing my declared major to mechanical engineering. He commended my decision and rated at 100 percent the applicability of my new intended major to his department. That's how I became an operations mechanical engineer. I had always earned good grades in chemistry, and I missed those classes. Chemistry was enjoyable to me, and I had a passion for it. But again, since I believed that everything that happened to me was for a greater purpose designed by God, I moved on and tried to think of mechanical engineering as the major about which I had always dreamed.

On Mother's Day 1977, I went to Marília to spend that weekend with my mother. My brother Silas, now working in a key-chain factory, asked if I would be willing to help him financially if he couldn't get admitted to a tuition-free state university. We bounced ideas off each other, back and forth, and talked a lot. Having faced the difficulties of working full-time and studying in the evening, I understood how hard it would be for him to qualify on the admission exams. It was a journey that demanded more time than he had to study.

I did want to help him, but we both knew that the public engineering schools in Sao Paulo, were by far the best ones in the country, and thus were harder to get into. Ironically they were and still are tuition-free, but the wealthy get in first because they can afford the best private middle schools and high schools in preparation for the admission exams. For the most part, the public universities are the best in Brazil, but private elementary, middle, and high schools are much better than the equivalent public schools.

Because of his full-time job, Silas did not have enough time to prepare for the college admission test, so he didn't think he would get into a free-tuition public school. He asked me whether I would be able to cover his expenses (tuition, room and board, and so on) for the duration of his undergrad studies, or at least until he could find a part-time job to cover such expenses. Having been forced to cut corners and at times practically starve myself to make it through college, I was no stranger to finding viable and cost-effective solutions. Rather than paying for Silas to go to a private college, I thought he'd be better off if he got into a public school. It would cost less, and he would get a better education and thus be more competitive in the workforce.

So my counteroffer to him was in the form of a question: "If you quit your job now, I give you monthly the net amount you make now, and you become a full-time senior high school student, could you get admitted to a public school of engineering?" Silas had always earned enviable grades at school, so his nodding in agreement came as no surprise. So we made the deal that Silas would resign from his job and spend those seven months before the admission exam devoting himself to full-time study.

We planned for success and reached it. Silas was admitted to one of the top three schools of engineering in the country, which happened to be a public, tuition-free school. He not only ranked high on the admission exam, but also graduated at the top of his class and was the valedictorian in 1982.

In 1977, Johnson & Johnson offered free English lessons, and all twenty-five employees of machine design were eligible. The company would pay for the course in full, and the classes would be held during working hours on the company *Throughout my life, I have been a "sign me up" person.* premises. Throughout my life, I have been a "sign me up" person. Anytime I see an opportunity to learn something or do something good, moral, and legal, I join in. For a year and a half, I had English classes on Tuesdays and Thursdays from 10:30 a.m. until noon. To this day, I believe that success is not necessarily linked to how much we know, but rather to how much we apply of what we know.

In June 1978, during the FIFA World Cup, after office hours I came across a Filipino who was there for the acceptance of a disposable diaper machine we had built for J&J in his country. He wanted to say something, but he thought that out of the two hundred and eighty people in that building, only Othmar Schildknecht, the Swiss director of engineering, spoke English. So in his effort to be friendly to people, this Filipino could only smile at them. I seized the opportunity to use the little English I knew, so instead of smiling back, I replied, "How are you?" Standing in the hallway, we engaged in a conversation. He told me he would like for Brazil to win the World Cup so that he could see the carnival parade on the streets.

As we were wrapping up our conversation, the engineering director walked by and overheard us. He called me into his office and told me of his surprise to hear that I already spoke that much English. He went on to tell me about a plan that he and his boss, the vice president, had to hire a local engineer who spoke English and was knowledgeable about machine design. They wanted this person to spend two years in the United States, working in the international development program to bring back to Brazil the expertise the company was missing and could not find locally. They had been searching for a while, even using an external recruiting firm, but given the specificity for which they were looking, no one had been found. Now that he knew how advanced my English was, he wondered if I would be open to taking on that challenge shortly after my graduation, which was six months away.

I needed to leave for my class, so we tabled the conversation and resumed it next day. Upon hearing more about the plan, I asked him to sign me up. After that, I didn't hear anything for a while, and I began to wonder whether they had either changed their minds or developed cold feet. But later I learned that the engineering director was already working with headquarters in New Jersey on a plan to be implemented shortly after my graduation. I began to take direct responsibility for developing concepts and designing equipment, without any help from a more senior professional. I felt good about that, and I noticed that I was operating at least one step above the level at which I was employed. That made me think that I should be promoted, but my supervisor—still that same acting manager—was not necessarily a person skilled in talent management. He probably wouldn't have agreed that I deserved a promotion and/or a raise in pay.

In the city newspaper, I saw a junior designer position with ENGESA, a local company specializing in manufacturing war tanks. I applied, passed the design skills test and medical clearance, and was offered the job at a salary 53 percent higher than what I was earning at Johnson & Johnson. The day after receiving the ENGESA job offer, I presented my resignation to Johnson & Johnson. The supervisor (acting manager) took my resignation letter to be approved by Mr. Schildknecht, the director of engineering, who called me into his office and asked why I wanted to leave the company.

This gentleman had a reputation for being abrupt, and most people avoided him, but I had no issues with him. As a matter of fact, I thought we got along well. Of the six thousand company employees on that site, I might have been the only one who never had any complaint about Mr. Schildknecht. I always saw him as a predictable person, which made it easier for me to work with him. If you got to know him, then you could anticipate his expectations, requirements, and preferences. He liked certain things, such as accurate answers. I've always preferred an honest and predictable person to a demagogue or hypocrite.

I never criticized the engineering director, and that bothered many people, especially my peers. They were waiting for the day when he would lose his temper and yell at me. I am happy to report that he yelled at me sooner than my worst enemy would have expected, and it happened in front of my twenty-four peers. Rather than working in individual offices, everyone in that department worked in an open space, like a hall, where everyone could hear any conversation. This director came to my workstation, stood just four feet away, and yelled at me at the top of his lungs. He wanted to know why the drawings of a piece of equipment on which I was working were late to manufacturing. There was a dead silence in the department

When he stopped yelling, and because I knew that he liked accurate answers, I told him that at three o'clock that same day, the last drawing would be at the machine shop floor for manufacturing. He continued his heated speech, mocking my answer and insinuating that the problem would now be solved in a few hours *only because* he had inquired about it. Calmly and respectfully, I explained to him that I had been working concurrently on two high-priority designs. In spite of whatever he had been told, that piece of equipment being discussed was moving ahead right on schedule.

His reaction will be with me forever. It also forever shut up my peers, none of whom ever mentioned again this episode of my getting yelled at by the gentleman. What was his reaction to what I had to say?

This gentleman told me loud and clear, so that everyone around me could hear, "Mr. Samuel, in no way, shape, or form, and under no circumstances do I consider you a lazy person, nor did I mean to insinuate that. I left my office and came in person to inquire about the status of this equipment design because I knew you were the one working on it. If any of your peers had been responsible for this design, instead of stopping by, I'd just have fired him." He thanked me for the answer and went back to his office. I was flattered by his final comments, but I also learned the lesson that no matter the level of aggressiveness coming your way, the best weapon for disarming an opponent is to speak the truth without fear.

No matter the level of aggressiveness coming your way, the best weapon for disarming an opponent is to speak the truth without fear.

That day I skipped lunch, and at 1:30 p.m. I handed the drawing blueprint to the machine shop. At 3:05 p.m. the director came to my workstation to

Never overpromise and underdeliver, because that will burn bridges and tarnish your reputation.

compliment me for the outcome, indicating that he had heard at the shop that the concept was robust and that this machine would be a great asset for the company. This means that he had gone directly to the workshop at three o'clock to check that I had delivered on commitment. If I can leave you a word of advice based on this experience, it would be to never overpromise and underdeliver because that will burn bridges and tarnish your reputation.

All of this happened a few days before I presented my resignation. On that day, when Mr. Schildknecht asked me why I wanted to leave the company, I did my best to be concise and provide accurate reasons why I was to leave Johnson & Johnson. The outcome of the conversation was that I left his office with a promotion and a salary that matched the external job offer. I felt valued for my professional competence, and I took this as something achieved through God-given talent and work recognition, rather than favoritism. Equally important was the fact that I felt treated not like a good negotiator, but like a decent, respected human being.

In December 1978, I finished my mechanical engineering operations course. As this was a BSME (bachelor in science of mechanical engineering), one of the programs being dropped that year by the Ministry of Education, I decided to further pursue a BME (bachelor's in mechanical engineering), which meant two more years attending classes

I have seen people who do not go anywhere because they are not brave enough to consider pleading for an exception, just because they fear their request will be denied.

every evening and on Saturdays from 8:00 a.m. to 4:00 p.m. I wanted to do that because I did not feel great about having a diploma in a field that no longer existed.

Company policy specified that employees were eligible for a scholarship for their first college degree, but it wouldn't hurt to ask for an exception for my second college degree. I wouldn't sit back and assume there would be no exception to the rule. I have seen people who do not go

I have never believed that the greatest rewards come through small efforts.

anywhere because they are not brave enough to consider pleading for an exception, just because they fear their request will be denied. I asked for—and my engineering director approved—full reimbursement of my tuition for this additional two-year program. It was an extensive and demanding program, but because I have never believed that the greatest rewards come through small efforts, I went the extra mile.

At work I now had a few projects on which I was the engineering leader, which meant I would be the engineering representative to attend multidepartment meetings with a scope beyond the engineering function. The brand manager in the marketing area led monthly meetings, which were attended by representatives from planning, engineering, procurement, packaging, R&D, manufacturing, and finance. These meetings broadened my horizons and helped me understand the big picture of our business, and I got to know more about all departments represented in such meetings.

Also in 1978 a new housing development sprang up in town, and I bought a lot with the intention of building a house in it. Soon after that, I bought my first car, a yellow, 1975-model, 1.3L Volkswagen Beetle. Now I owned a car, I was doing well at work, and I had a gorgeous girlfriend, but the most important thing was the spiritual peace I enjoyed by exercising my daily walk with God. The head banging was behind me.

In late 1978 Yutaka Hayashi, a Japanese engineer, was hired to manage the machine design department. I was excited to work with someone from a different culture than the Brazilians, Swiss, Mongols, and Germans with whom I had interacted previously. During his first three months with the company, this gentleman called me into his office and told me he would recommend my promotion to designer. He went over my deliverables, academic background, and upward mobility, and told me that I was overqualified and underpaid for my senior draftsman title. Based on his understanding of the job description, the work I was doing was by no means second to that of any designer in the group. Trying not to read into this more than what I was being told, I thanked him for his feedback. At the age of twenty-two I became the youngest designer ever in that group. Life was good and my career was on a fast track.

In July 1979, Celia and I got engaged. We made plans to get married after I finished engineering school, which was on track for graduation in December 1980.

At the church I attended, I was starting to emerge more and more as a potential leader. In fact, I was invited to fill in as the acting youth pastor for the six-thousand-person church, which meant transferring to the main church downtown. With that I had visibility in church to thousands of people, and I was humbled by that opportunity to serve. These volunteer activities at church projected me as a speaker and a person of whom people had high expectations, but it also meant that if I slipped, thousands of eyes would be watching. I now had a busy schedule with church because I would reach out and join forces to work across denominations on projects that would be of mutual benefit. I was also invited to preach at many church-organized events.

13

Challenges? Bring Them On!

As a designer, I led my own projects with a trainee designer and a draftsman working for me. My first task was to interface with the requester (internal customer) to understand the requirements, and then I would work on developing the equipment concept and general assembly before passing it on to my team for designing the parts for manufacturing. One of the requests that came to me was to develop and build a machine for research and development pilot plant use in making sanitary napkin prototypes. The machine had to be modular and flexible, offer quick changeover to different product formats, and be versatile enough to accommodate a variety of product concepts still under development. This R&D equipment was the kind of development I liked to have because there was nothing similar to it on the market and I had to start from scratch. The project enabled me to interact with many people at the R&D center, including the vice president, a Canadian citizen originally from Guadeloupe.

People aren't valued for what they know, but rather for how they use what they know.

One day I needed to communicate some critical points on the pilot machine that R&D had ordered, so I seized the opportunity to validate my own saying, that "People aren't valued for what they know, but rather for how they use what they know." My proficiency in English was intermediate at best, but to make sure that the foreigners accountable for the project would fully understand definitions I needed from them, I wrote them an internal letter in English. It's amazing how this letter opened up opportunities for me in the organization. You see, I could have been shy about writing in English because of the danger of making mistakes, ridiculing myself, and burning opportunities for advancement. But after I weighed the pros and cons, my courage was greater than my fear, so I sent the letter in English.

If you don't use up the little you know, you might never find where help can come from.

Even if you know only a little bit, use everything you know. If you don't use up the little you know, you might never find where help can come from, so that you continue to expand your knowledge. Some people unknowingly become their own barriers to advancement and growth, ultimately not achieving their dreams because they do not apply what they know. They are dominated by a fear of failure and their assumption that they will always fail. The higher the risk, the greater the reward. If you do not use up your knowledge, what's the advantage of knowing it? If you have the knowledge to do good things that will help people around you and mankind in general, then use it.

The higher the risk, the greater the reward.

After the (concept maker) pilot machine was built, R&D needed an engineer to lead what would be the pilot plant where the machine would be used. They asked me to help with the recruiting, and after a few weeks without any success, they asked me for a recommendation of someone who could fill that position. Shooting from the hip, I asked, "What about me?"

The R&D leadership had mixed feelings about my recommendation because they knew the engineering director would not willingly let me make that move. He had plans for me in machine design, which included sending me to a two-year training program in the United States. As much as they feared the conflict, however, they liked the idea of having me come over to R&D and take over their pilot plant.

Just when my dream of living in the USA for a couple of years was about to come true, I was making a decision that would throw that opportunity out the window by moving to R&D. Why? I was twenty-three years old and ambitious in terms of professional growth. I suspected that spending two years in the USA and then returning to Brazil to be the lead machine designer, eventually the machine designer supervisor, was a once-in-a-lifetime opportunity. The problem was that becoming the best machine designer was not necessarily what I had in mind for myself. As much as I loved the idea, R&D was more enticing and could open multiple doors into future management positions. I never had the short term as my greatest goal.

For R&D, I was the ideal candidate. They needed someone who would understand and further develop the equipment I had designed for them— and who could do that better than the *I never had the short term as my greatest goal* person who created it? Soon, however, R&D's fears came to fruition. The engineering director did not agree with the transfer, so Human Resources was called in to mediate. As a young professional, being fought over by a vice president and a director made me feel good, so I raised my price.

R&D wanted me to tell engineering that making the move had been my idea. Though that was true, they wanted the burden to be all on my shoulders so there would *Being fearless in negotiations is not a bad thing.* be less resistance from engineering. After all, who would want to hold back someone who wants to be somewhere else? I agreed to do that, but I wanted a double promotion rather than moving up just one level. They agreed, and a tug-of-war ensued for a couple of months. But in October 1980, I was transferred to R&D with a double promotion and a 30 percent salary increase, just two months shy of finishing my degree in mechanical engineering. The lesson learned was that I needed to know what I wanted for my career, but I also had to have a clear picture of how much I was worth in terms of salary. Being fearless in negotiations is not a bad thing.

For me it is important to recognize who deserves the credit when I gave things full credit.

The correlation between my spiritual and professional growth was strong, and for every success milestone I gave God full credit.

There's a song that says, "Hold on to God's hand." I did just that, aware that his hand was always stretched out to me. My happiness was visible. Although the norm seems to be for people to seek God in moments of despair—and I will not deny that I have done that myself in tough times—I made it a habit to stay close to God when things were going well. Also, he can always find a way to improve on what I consider the best. For me, it is important to recognize who deserves the credit when everything goes right.

In R&D I was operating two levels above my previous job and expectations were high, so I tried as hard as I could to make sure they were all met. My only question was how people who had no technical knowledge or understanding of what I was doing could be fair in their as- *If there's one thing I've always done well, it is to know how to be marketable.* sessments for rating my performance. My solution was to assume that it was my role to make sure they *could* understand not only the complexity of my tasks but also the value I was bringing, and I think I did that reasonably well.

If there's one thing I've always done well, it is to know how to be marketable, though I never felt overpaid. My work in R&D was quite different, since I was no longer designing equipment. Instead I led prototype development and *If you do not want anyone to envy you, then don't do anything well.* defined R&D requirements to engineering. Some of the things they asked of me made no sense, and some of the suggestions were technically more expensive and less effective. Again I found myself on stage to prove to the leadership which solution would be best, while still learning how to navigate through the R&D maze.

It did not take long for me to stand out in R&D and become sought after for engineering solutions, even to R&D areas outside of my scope of responsibilities. However, there is no such a thing as a free lunch, and my success came with a price tag. As I progressed along my R&D learning curve, I could feel envious remarks and words of discouragement. But I didn't care, because they were not coming from people who were good role models, but rather from people stuck in their careers. So my advice to you is that if you do not want anyone to envy you, then don't do anything well.

Envious people suffer because they think of opportunities as being finite, like a pizza. If you eat every slice, they envy you. They don't realize that there are enough pizzas for everyone. The one you ate wasn't the only pizza in the world! Sometimes I think envious people don't actually want to have what you have.

> *Sometimes I think envious people don't actually want to have what you have. Instead, they just don't want you to have what you have.*

Instead, they just don't want *you* to have what you have. Up to that point in my career, I had been treated fairly well by the German, the Swiss, the Mongol, the Japanese, and the Canadian, but facing my own countrymen was a little bit of an extra challenge. The gringos did not care to be challenged; actually they liked to have their point of view challenged, but some of the Brazilians would take it personally and await opportunities for retaliation.

As I began to be required to assist the R&D function outside of my own department, my supervisor was somewhat troubled because he had no direct control over my actions. Honestly, I did not care; he never understood equipment engineering, and I did not want his opinion anyway. Having failed in every attempt to tell me how to do my job, he tried to exercise control by demoralizing and humiliating me. Do not take me wrong—I did every project my supervisor asked me to do, and I was never disrespectful. However, I did not trade my equipment concepts for his because his made no sense. In his attempt to derail me from my focused and fast-tracked career, he reopened some old wounds by saying things that used to hurt me when I was a child. What did he do? He told me that because of the color of my skin, I would never advance past the level of scientist. The profile of successful people within Johnson & Johnson was that of a blond male with green eyes.

He was probably a rookie at making racist remarks, whereas I, despite being fairly young, had often faced discriminatory comments and bullying because of my skin color. The difference was that I had learned how to eat the fish and spit out the bones. I ignored his remarks because at the end of the day, he was the one troubled. In contrast, I was just having a great time at work doing what I was doing. He would continue to be my supervisor for another couple of years, and he possessed the preferred blond hair and green eyes, but by no means would I consider him a successful leader. A true leader respects people for their skills and ability to do the job, and a true leader would never hold back anyone because of the color of their skin. I was silent and thoughtful while my supervisor described his own stereotype as being the profile for success, but he was far from being a benchmark leader whose steps I would ever try to follow.

Building a family was an important thing for me, and in March 1981, I received a wonderful gift. Second to Jesus Christ, the best thing that has ever happened to me was the gift that God sent me wrapped in a bridal dress. In front of fifteen hundred guests, Celia and I got married, and that same pastor who had baptized me officiated at my wedding ceremony.

While still a scientist, I always tried to work closely with my colleagues and understand their needs outside of work. A colleague was going through a challenging time, and one day I invited *"Actions speak louder than words,"* her to lunch so that we could talk. One of the managers asked his secretary to calmly call my wife at home and let her know that I had just left for a motel room with a female coworker. My wife answered the phone and heard what the woman had to say. Then Celia thanked the woman for the call, but said she was married to a godly man and did not believe what she was hearing. The woman insisted it was true, so my wife told her that my coworker and I were not in a motel room. Instead, we were sitting with Celia in our home dining room, where the three of us were having lunch. My wife then passed the phone over to me, so the secretary would know it was not a bluff, but indeed I was home. Unfortunately there are people, especially the envious ones, who make this kind of judgment about other people's lives, assuming that everybody is just like them.

As I started to advance socially and economically, I was

gradually coming to the conclusion that discrimination was actually against the poor. I was born black, poor, and evangelical, which in Brazil made me a triple minority, and I had faced my share of challenges and discrimination for each of those three characteristics. My response to discrimination has always been to prove the discriminator wrong by achieving success beyond that of the discriminator. As the saying goes, "Actions speak louder than words." Through my actions, I would shut them off, but I never made any effort to retaliate or try to prove that the discriminator was wrong, let alone sue for money.

I was always happy just the way God made me. I do not believe he made a mistake when picking my skin color.

The only thing that really irritated me was when someone tried to comfort me by saying that I was not black but rather a mulatto. I never needed solace from anyone in this area because I was always happy just the way God made me. I do not believe he made a mistake when picking my skin color. When facing discrimination, I always responded that I was glad to have my job and that I would do my best to advance my career based solely on merit.

Some of the people I came across were so weak that, having no strength to prove their own capability for advancement, they would spend time and energy trying to stop me, which was a terrible mistake. The only way they had to attack me was to use my skin color as a hindrance to my success and hope that would discourage me. I *never* let that thought stick to me. I was in it to win, so it would take much more than that to drain my motivation. Little did they know that, in fact, I used their attacks as yet another motivational factor.

Absolutely everything that happens to me occurs only with God's consent.

My tranquility always came—and still comes—from my assumption that absolutely everything that happens to me occurs only with God's consent. I am immensely grateful to God. He never gave me everything for which I asked, but he *did* give me everything I needed and everything he wanted to give me.

In the church also I emerged as a leader, and in mid-1981 I was appointed superintendent of the Sunday school at the church head-quarters of the Assemblies of God in São José dos Campos, at that time with six hundred students. I also continued as the assistant youth leader for that denomination.

In early 1982, I had a new and indescribable experience. Celia and I had the privilege and blessing to be parents for the first time. God presented us with a beautiful girl, who was easy to identify in the nursery because her beauty stood out. Everyone who visited and the employees of the hospital said that our daughter was the prettiest child in the hospital nursery. I certainly hope they did not say that to each and every parent! Erika Kathryn was born amid a risk of eclampsia, but thank God everything went well with mother and child. The dynamics in our home would forever change.

My parents became grandparents for the first time. As often their schedules allowed, they traveled the 340 miles to see the newborn and stay at our home. After the birth of my daughter Erika, my sister Sonia came to live with us. That was a great help to Celia, making it easier for her to finish her college education in social sciences.

Erika was eighteen months old when I had to take a plane for a two-week business trip. After a week away, however, I had to return home for the weekend because on the fourth day I was gone, my little baby had gone on a hunger strike. Doctors could not find anything wrong with her, but when I got home and gave her a hug and a kiss, her hunger strike was over. She had never gone a day without seeing her father. Now the strike was over and so was the breastfeeding. On Sunday night I traveled again, but she was content after having me there with her for two days. If I ever had any doubts about the importance of my paternal role and presence, Erika would erase those doubts.

That same year my youngest brother, Dario Junior, moved to São José dos Campos. After years of studying in the evening and working full-time as a toolmaker, he had completed high school and made plans to work full-time while studying engineering. For a couple of reasons, he didn't have a hard time in getting settled. First, over a seven-year period as the oldest brother, I had opened the way and was financially positioned to help him get started. Second, unlike me he did not have the job of "cleaner" recorded on his work permit, but rather a two-year experience as a toolmaker. Dario Junior moved in with Celia, Erika, Sonia, and me. In a matter of weeks, he was hired by Petrobras and soon started to earn enough income to be financially independent from me.

In 1982, at the age of twenty-six I would become the youngest minister of my church. That wasn't the first time that I had been *the youngest*, because I had also become the youngest designer at Johnson & Johnson. In January 1983 I was elected to the steward board of church, and I was the youngest on the presiding board, occupying the post of first secretary. On the occasion of the president's absence, I would lead the church services, with fifteen hundred people in attendance at the main church downtown (Assembly of God, Rua Conselheiro Rodrigues Alves 417, São José dos Campos-SP). The way I describe things that happened to me may sound a little arrogant to those who do not know me personally. With no false modesty, I never understood how the grace of God could be so great in my life. Indeed, it was all done by his grace. None of this would have happened if it had depended on my merits alone.

14

The Promise

Changes are constant in any organization, and I went through quite a few of them. With the economic crisis in Brazil in the early eighties, the company downsized the staff a few times, and for many employees, the anticipation of layoffs was a nightmare. It was a time in my career when I felt I was going nowhere, but rather was stuck in a relatively low-level job compared with my expectations. Finding a job elsewhere was unlikely; jobs were few and far between because every business was facing the same challenges.

During the country's economic crisis, I walked into a Christian bookstore and came across a book titled *You Can Become the Person You Want to Be*, by Robert Schuller. The title of the book caught my attention, and after flipping through a couple of pages, I bought it. That book ended up helping me more than I ever could imagine. Second to the Bible, it became the book that has influenced my life the most. I chose to believe the lessons in the book, as well as the recommendations on how to overcome tough times.

This book presented several examples on how people who would otherwise have failed emerged through faith and persistence to overcome what some would consider insurmountable barriers. Because I believed what I was reading, I applied it to my life and harvested positive results. At first I did not believe that my stalled corporate career could be advanced by reading a book written by a pastor. Written by Robert Schuler, the book presents stories of winning through faith and determination, and those lessons learned seemed to have a direct application to my life at that time.

A couple of months later, I went back to the bookstore, bought a half dozen copies of that same book, and presented them as gifts to some of my coworkers. I think some of them had a prejudice against reading a book written by a pastor, but the one or two people who read it applied the lessons and saw the difference it made to their lives. To my surprise, one colleague came to me and returned the book I had given her, explaining that she would not read it because she wouldn't believe any of the content anyway. Unfortunately she missed a great opportunity to improve her standard of living because of her prejudice, as later she told me her main reason for not reading the book was that it had been written by a pastor. Her career never progressed beyond the level she was at in the 1980s. You should never miss an opportunity to learn, overcome, and be happy because you let prejudice get in the way.

You should never miss an opportunity to learn, overcome, and be happy because you let prejudice get in the way.

I vividly remember the day a green-eyed, blond coworker told me what had happened to him. Feeling under the weather, he had gone to the company clinic, where a black person asked how she could help him. My coworker explained that he was there to see the doctor. When she identified herself as the medical doctor on duty, his immediate reaction was to mock her. He thought she was pulling his leg because he had a hard time believing that a black woman could be a medical doctor in Brazil. Suddenly a nurse entered the room and addressed the black woman as Doctor Therezinha. Realizing that the black woman was indeed a doctor, but unable to get past his prejudice, my coworker left without seeing the doctor.

Prejudice can actually be more damaging to the offender than to the person discriminated against. I know that from my own experience. When I'm discriminated against, I never argue or try to

Prejudice can actually be more damaging to the offender than to the one discriminated against.

prove the other person wrong. Instead, I reaffirm to myself who I am and what I am capable of. Do not waste time insisting on recognition and acceptance from people who will not change their minds no matter what you do.

In 1984 the company downsized for the third year in a row. Weeks before the layoff, a coworker and close friend approached me with some news. After ensuring that I would not betray her confidence, because that could get her in trouble, she asked me to take a deep breath and stay calm. Then

Do not waste time insisting on recognition and acceptance from people who will not change their minds no matter what you do.

she confided in me that she had heard from a secure source that my supervisor had put my name on the layoff list. I was shocked because that supervisor was new to the company and was having difficulties in learning his job and leading his group. I thanked her for trusting me with something so confidential and assured her that I was fine. Then I told her I was going to have a conversation with the man at the top. She thought I meant the vice president, but I said no. Then she stared at me with wide eyes, thinking I meant to speak with the president. So I cut the questions short, pointed to the sky, and said that I would talk with God.

Finding another job would be a herculean challenge because so many companies were reducing their workforce. I couldn't afford to lose my job, especially back then when there was no unemployment benefit. I had a little daughter to raise and a mortgage to pay, and I was the only source of income for the household. On my way back home that day, I couldn't help but think of the days when I had first arrived in that city and how hard it had been to find a job. When I got home, I kissed my wife and daughter and closed the bedroom door behind me.

On my knees, I talked to God and told him what I had heard. Then I told him that I was going to open the Bible, and that I would like for him to put my finger on the page, chapter, and verse where he had an answer to my situation. I opened the Bible with my finger on these two verses from Ezekiel 17:23–24: "On the mountain heights of Israel I will plant it; it will produce branches and bear fruit and become a splendid cedar. Birds of every kind will nest in it; they will find shelter in the shade of its branches. All the trees of the forest will know that I the Lord bring down the tall tree and make the low tree grow tall. I dry up the green tree and make the dry tree flourish. I the Lord have spoken, and I will do it."

The first time I read these verses, I did not understand how they provided an answer to my despair at the prospect of losing my job. My problem was no different from that of many people today. We go to God expecting to receive a handout, when he indeed does as Luke 6:38 says, "A good measure, pressed down, shaken together and running over, will be poured into your lap."

I read these verses from Ezekiel again, asking God to help me understand and decode his answer—and He did. The interpretation came this way to me:

We usually seek God to calm the storm around us, but in this case he calmed the storm inside me.

On the mountain heights of Israel I will plant it [You will ascend to the highest position in R&D]; it will produce branches and bear fruit and become a splendid cedar [You will lead a recognized organization with many talents]. Birds of every kind will nest in it; they will find shelter in the shade of its branches [People from multiple nations will be in your organization and you will help them]. All the trees of the forest will know that I the Lord bring down the tall tree [Everyone will know that I take people down from their high positions] and make the low tree grow tall [and raise those in low positions]. I dry up the green tree and make the dry tree flourish [I fire your supervisor and promote you]. I the Lord have spoken, and I will do it. [I, your God, have told you this and will surely do it]. (Ezekiel 17:23–24)

I wiped my tears, washed my face, and joined my wife for dinner, comforted and confident that God had taken care of that situation. When the person who had confided in me about my termination saw me the next day, she was puzzled by my demeanor. I didn't seem shaken or down. If fact, I didn't have any worries at all, because deep inside I knew God was in control—and I let her know that. We usually seek God to calm the storm around us, but in this case he calmed the storm inside me.

Then came the fateful Friday when the layoff would take place. I had no reason not to believe the interpretation of the Bible verses God had given me, so I faced it just like another ordinary day at work. As I expected, because that's what God had told me, my supervisor was fired and his job was split into two positions. I got one of them, which put me in line for a future promotion if I performed to expectations

In addition to all the responsibilities I had for family, work, and church, I was given the additional task of presenting the church radio program every Sunday night from eleven o'clock to midnight. Not that I had spare time, but I was used to being busy. I also moonlighted as a teacher in a vocational high school on Tuesday and Friday nights. This was a good experience that led to being a college professor later on, also moonlighting.

It was also in the early eighties that the Full Gospel Business Men Fellowship International (FGBMFI) arrived in São José dos Campos. I joined and became one of the directors, a speaker, and an instructor. In that cross-denominational fellowship, I came to know some of the most talented executives in the world. For eleven years starting in 1983, I was fully engaged with the FGBMFI—first locally, then regionally, and finally nationally.

Among other activities, the FGBMFI, founded by Demos Shakarian in the USA, organized dinners with entrepreneurs, businessmen, and businesswomen in attendance. During dinner, Fellowship members or invited guests would share their

I inherited from my parents the principle that it is more worthy to serve the church than to be served by the church.

testimonials, which normally demonstrated a strong correlation between Christian faith and succeeding in business. At the end of the testimonial, invitees were given the opportunity to make a decision for Jesus Christ. My testimony was personally shared in several states of Brazil, and some listeners considered it so effective that they suggested that I put it in a book to share more broadly. As a result of their suggestion, you are now reading my testimonial.

I could see an interesting correlation between my professional career advancements and the increased scope of responsibilities in my church activities. They were so connected that I'd say one depended on the other, though I never knew why.

When the churches in other cities in that region (Vale do Paraiba–Sao Paulo) heard about my preaching, invitations to speak started to come, beyond what I had availability to do. It felt great to be able to encourage and help so many people through faith live a full life, but I could not honor all invitations because of my full-time job. The common practice was for the inviting church to give the invited speaker a donation to cover at least his travel expenses, and sometimes they would offer more than that, as a token of their appreciation for the time and effort. Every time I was offered such a donation, I respectfully declined it and suggested that they use that money at that church for advancing the kingdom of God. Some would insist, but I would tell them that I had a full-time job at Johnson & Johnson. My deal with God was that as long as I had that job, I would not accept any donation from any church, but rather serve as a volunteer at my own expense. I inherited from my parents the principle that it is more worthy to serve the church than to be served by the church.

We also need a sponsor and a mentor to get the visibility and support to grow.

My professional career was advancing at a good pace, and I saw in it the fulfillment of the verses I read in Ezekiel about raising the low tree and bringing down the high tree. For six years I had been at the same job level, but time seemed to be catching up.

One of the things I learned, and now pass on to youngsters, is that when considering a career move or a job change, we should never move into a job that does not allow for leveraging a good part of our past experiences. There's got to be an overlap, like in walking. You stand on your past experience leg and step forward with your other leg. We do not take both feet off the ground at the same time when we walk. Past experience ensures performance in the new job, and new learning allows for advancement. When the leg forward is still and new experiences are mastered, then you move ahead with the other leg into some new learning.

When I moved from engineering to R&D, I went to the pilot plant operation where 60 percent of the job was engineering, so that I could leverage my past experience while learning about new product development. However, that alone does not assure success because we also need a sponsor and a mentor to get the visibility and support to grow. I did not have a mentor.

After learning about product development, I no longer depended solely on my knowledge of processes, and then I could move toward new knowledge. Again, as in walking, we take one foot off the ground at a time. With one leg we stand, and with the other we advance. See each leg as a group of different skills, and see that no one walks by putting both legs forward at the same time. Remember this the next time you consider changing jobs. You can take both feet off the ground when you jump, but a jump is a single intermittent event, whereas walking is a process. A career is a process—not an event.

One of the brightest people I know has decided to move from being an engineer to being an attorney. What did she do? Being a mechanical engineer, she became a patent attorney, which meant that her engineering knowledge was used in the assessment of process patent applications. She leveraged past experience and, in her mid-thirties, she progressed enough to make it to the vice president level and then associate general counsel in one of the largest multinational companies.

From 1985 to 1987, I attended business graduate school. Halfway through that program, Celia and I were blessed with a second daughter. We were all happy, and big sister Erika, who was fast approaching her fifth birthday, could not take her eyes off her younger sister, Renate.

15

Climbing the Corporate Ladder

At work I did not feel I was receiving the appropriate recognition for my technical contributions or progressing at the speed I should. I had to work on the missing link, but I didn't quite know what it was. Because attending multidepartmental meetings had provided me a broader scope and exposure, I seized that opportunity to shorten the distance to marketing by working closer with the brand manager who led these meetings.

My director had the high-potential folks list, but I never knew if I was on that list. The fact is that I was on my God's list and that kept me going.

I was the lead scientist for one of the two most important projects in the ten-person research department. Maria, marketing's senior manager, consulted me about the workload and whether I could handle both of the top two projects. As the project I had led was about to be completed and the other project could leverage a lot of my learning, given their similarity, I said yes. She explained that for the project I was leading, they knew exactly what was going on and they were never left in the dark for lack of information. On the other project, led by my peer, she never got needed updates and her calls were not always returned. So Maria was going to talk to my boss, the R&D director, and ask him to give me the other project as well.

When she conferred with him, however, he denied her request. Maria was a persistent woman who believed in her judgment, so she asked her boss, the marketing director, who was my director's peer, to intervene on her behalf. The marketing director had the conversation with the R&D director, but to no avail. The marketing and R&D directors reported to the same person, the managing director, who was asked by the marketing director to help in getting me to lead that project. The managing director then told my boss, the R&D director, to give me leadership of that project—and so he did. I successfully led both projects to completion. I knew that was my best chance up to that moment and I could not mess it up, so I put my best foot forward.

My upbringing had taught me how to treat everyone with dignity and respect, regardless of their social class. I believe this naturally humble attitude, combined with the high quality of my work, brought me to the attention of the marketers who in those days were influential in the company's decisions. Humility always wins over pride. "Pride goes before destruction, a haughty spirit before a fall" (Proverbs 16:18).

Humility always wins over pride.

As I continued elbowing my way up in the organization, Susan, a brand manager, came to see me about projects that she wanted to implement in the brand she managed. She was the marketing brand manager, and I was the product development scientist for that same brand. I dissuaded her from doing those projects she had in mind, instead serving up others about which I had long thought. Susan was—and still is—a pragmatic person who likes to understand all details before buying into an idea. Based on learning from previous projects and consumer insights on unmet needs, in my effort to convince her I told her that if she were to successfully launch the product changes I was proposing, I would envision that success taking her up to senior manager of marketing.

About a year later, Susan set up a lunch meeting and wanted to take me to a fancy restaurant. I had not seen the marketing share data, and I had no idea if the projects I had suggested had been a success or a fiasco. In any case, I was prepared to question the marketing execution because technically those products we had just launched were far superior to the ones they had replaced. As we noshed on appetizers, Susan thanked me for the products I had developed, shared the lift in market share, and reminded me that I had told her she would be promoted. Then she disclosed that her promotion to marketing senior manager would be announced the following week. I first congratulated her and then laughed at the fact that we had launched only two of the three products we had jointly planned.

My heart had been converted to the gospel of Jesus Christ, so I tried to ensure that my wallet was equally converted. I once heard that it is much easier to identify a true Christian through his bank statement or checkbook than through his Bible.

I decided to continue investing in real estate, and then in the late eighties I made an offer to buy a lot in a middle-class neighborhood in the city where I lived. I wanted to pay for it with cash, but I had only 90 percent of the asking price. I extended an offer to buy the property, but my efforts failed. The real estate agents conveyed back to me the message that the sellers would not take less than the asking price.

The next day, a Saturday, I went to a church leadership meeting. The pastor of one of our satellite churches reported that the church he led had severe roof leakage and the whole roof needed replacing. The rainy season was approaching, and, in his words, sometimes he had the impression that there would be more water coming in through the roof than running through the downspouts. He suggested that all the churches represented in that meeting spearhead a one-month campaign to gather donations for the roof replacement.

Pastor Miguel Cornelio was on stage presenting the total roof replacement cost. As a church steward, I would normally be working for the church during such a meeting, which meant walking all around the sanctuary where we met. So I walked over to him and, in a whisper, told him not to start any campaign. Then I handed him a personal check to cover the whole roof replacement. He was the only person who knew what I was doing. Most people thought of me as the timekeeper at those meetings, so they probably thought I had just told him to cut his talk short and take his seat. In a sense, I guess I had just done that, Instead of returning to his seat, however, he starting crying. For a couple of minutes, he kept more than a hundred people curious about what exactly I had said to him.

On Monday morning the real estate agent called me at work to let me know that over the weekend, the sellers had thought about my 90 percent offer and decided to accept it. Because I had paid for the church roof, I then had only 70 percent of the asking price. I explained to the real estate agent what had happened and the reason why I could no longer buy that property. To my amazement, half an hour later the agent called to tell me that if I was still interested in that lot, the sellers would close the deal for the money I had—just 70 percent of the asking price. You see, I had given up on acquiring that lot because I really had no more money to offer, but God had other plans. He had tested my obedience in giving, so that I could then receive from him an even greater blessing. And the blessings did not stop there. Two months later, I sold the land for a reasonable profit. From that episode, I learned that in order to be blessed, we need to bless others first. Giving unselfishly is like sowing and expecting the harvest.

In 1990 I was appointed to lead the Assembly of God's Jardim Satelite in the city of São José dos Campos, the largest sub-congregation in town. Though I was a minister, I had never led a church, and I was replacing a full-time pastor who had available time to serve the congregation's needs. I served as a volunteer while leading that three-hundred-person church. It was a learning experience, and by the grace of God, both the congregation and I had a blessed time.

In order to be blessed, we need to bless others first.

While I was leading that church, a fellow pastor was invited to preach one Sunday night. After his sermon, he gave an altar call for people who had a prayer request, either for themselves or for a friend or relative. I was surprised to see my nine-year-old daughter, Erika, kneeling at the altar. I did not ask her reasons for being there because I assumed that if she wanted me to know, she would tell me. For more than six months, Erika had been in physical therapy for scoliosis, with no improvement identified by her doctor. She was scheduled to continue physical therapy for a few more months, so the doctor could assess whether that would be of any help to her. A week after the altar call, Erika had x-rays and a follow-up assessment with her doctor. This time the x-ray indicated that she no longer had scoliosis. On the way home, she told us that because there had been no improvement with the therapy, she had answered the altar call and asked God for divine healing of her backbone. Her prayer request was answered and she was completely healed.

Several more organizational changes took place at work, and every time a change was implemented, either my scope of responsibilities or my title would be upgraded. Admittedly I had a covenant with God, and believe me, there's no better partner than God. Financially I made some progress, including buying a better car and additional real estate in town. Because I came from a humble and poor family, I was never big on luxury or living lavishly, but I was good at creating reserves for an adverse time, should it ever come.

When it rains, it pours. In 1986 I was promoted to senior scientist, in 1988 to supervisor, in 1989 to area manager, and in 1990 to department manager. Four promotions within a four-year period was something unheard of. For people who had known that I was about to be fired in 1984, it really was a major course correction for the good. But I gave God credit for guiding me through the tough times. I was constantly aware that I needed to cast all my cares upon God and trust him, but I also did my part. If he does his part but I do not do mine, I won't go anywhere. What God told Joshua also applied to me: "Be strong and of good courage" (Joshua 1:9).

I had the opportunity to travel throughout Brazil with the sales force, to attend product launch meetings where my role was to introduce the new product to them. Being a familiar face to the sales team, I became the site host whenever they came to the R&D labs and manufacturing plant to refresh their knowledge or for business orientation. I

I had to be mindful of not becoming a poor photograph, and by that I mean one that is overexposed and underdeveloped.

had fairly good visibility, and if there's one thing I always liked, it was exposure. However, I had to be mindful of not becoming a *poor photograph*, and by that I mean one that is overexposed and under-developed. Some people are intimidated by having to be on stage, face an audience, and speak in public. But ever since, at the age of nine, my father put me on stage to preach, I have always enjoyed being in evidence. If there is a brick, I'll climb on it and give a speech.

In the late eighties I began traveling internationally, visiting countries in Latin America, North America, and Europe. Now I was showing my face in countries other than Brazil, either for technical assistance or training. That's when I began studying German and Italian because I wanted to talk to people in their own language whenever possible. Not only that, but I'm competitive and learning languages is one of my strengths, so language acquisition could be an advantage or even a tiebreaker for better opportunities, both within and possibly outside the company for which I worked.

By the way, that former supervisor—the one who told me that because of my dark skin color, I would never go past the scientist level with that company—now worked for me, and I was three levels higher than when he said that. As his manager, I could have thrown it back in his face and told him that mulattos with brown eyes were also part of the success profile in that company. But my focus was, and has always been, on my own improvement and advancement, rather than on looking back or seeking revenge. In the forty-seven years that Johnson & Johnson had been in Brazil, nobody of my skin color had ever risen to such positions. That fact encouraged me to be the first, so that I could pave the way for others who might otherwise have been discouraged by believing in words that left them feeling down.

> "...my focus was and has always been on my own improvement and advancement rather than looking back or seeking revenge."

In R&D I was now managing a group of eleven professionals with degrees either in polymeric materials engineering or chemical engineering. Technically they were much more competent than I was, but because I had dedicated myself to strategy and leadership, that allowed me to rise even in an area where my academic background was not necessarily the most applicable.

As God blessed me, I would in return bless others, starting with my parents for all they had done for me. So we, their children, built them a new, bigger, and better house.

16

Insurmountable Challenges

The fact that God was always with me did not mean I would not face tough challenges, but instead assured that he would see me through the challenges. You see, God never promised a life without difficulties. As Jesus Christ said, "In this world you will have trouble, but take Heart! I have overcome the world" (John 16:33 NIV).

During my 1992 performance review, my director told me that I had reached the highest possible level within the company for a dark-skinned person. My rating was the highest possible score, for the second year in a row. I do not know why he said that—I never wanted to know—but that was not the first time a direct boss had told me that my skin color would limit my career growth opportunities in that company. One thing I knew, however, was that I should ignore his remarks and continue to focus on doing my job to the best of my ability. To help get past his comments, I paraphrased Jesus Christ and said to myself, "Father, forgive my director because he does not know what he says."

Accustomed to discrimination and racial comments, I was determined not to discuss with anyone what I had just been told. But my director seemed so proud of what he had told me that he could not keep it to himself, so he shared it with some of his peers. One of his peers came to see me, but I realized that person only wanted to use the situation for personal gain over my boss. He wasn't sympathetic to my situation—not that I ever needed anyone to feel sorry for me or take up my cause. I was able to defend myself, and I never wanted anyone to speak on my behalf concerning this matter. Because my director had a big mouth, the word was out about his comments to me. But I had no reason to be ashamed or feel victimized because I had entrusted my destiny to God and I feared God alone.

With my social and economic progression in 1993, my wife and I decided to build our dream house in the soon-to-be—according to the developer and macro plan—most affluent gated community in that city of four hundred thousand. I bought the lot, paid the architects to design the house we wanted, and hired a builder, Angra Engenharia, who was renowned for building luxury homes in upscale neighborhoods. As part of the down payment on the construction of the house, I used a lot that I owned in the second-best gated community in town and some cash I had saved for this house.

While still working on the foundation of the house, the builder went bankrupt. The company owner, Paulo Ricardo Ferreira, was nowhere to be found and supposedly had moved to the southernmost state in Brazil. I was left with construction that had barely started and a loss in today's money equivalent to one hundred thousand dollars. For me, a person always happy to have been blessed beyond measure by the God of my faith, that was a major setback. I assessed my loss and calculated that it would take five years to save the amount that I had just lost, and thus eight years to build a house I was expecting to build in three years. Needless to say, I was extremely disappointed with my decision to put down such a huge amount of money. The worst disappointment was knowing that the builder already knew he was going bankrupt when he signed the contract with me. He had just used me to get that hundred thousand dollars and hit the road, never to be found.

What did I do? I could not blame God, so I proceeded to give testimony of God's love and how he blesses people even when they do not deserve it. Although the builder gained and I lost, God—who sees the end from the beginning—was in control, though I'll admit that at times it required extra effort to keep my face and faith up. It's like the story of the caterpillar turning into a butterfly. What the larva (caterpillar) calls the end of the world, the butterfly calls the beginning of life. It is easy to be thankful to God when things in our lives are settling in gracefully, but now that I was in dire straits, I had an opportunity to remember Job and praise the God who gives and takes away. And so I did, despite that one hundred thousand dollar loss being greater than two years of my gross compensation at the time.

Construction was put on hold for lack of funds. I often spoke with God about that uncomfortable situation, but I never showed dejection. After all, as I had read in the Bible, "If you faint in the day of adversity, your strength is too small" (Proverbs 24:10).

What the larva (caterpillar) calls the end of the world, the butterfly calls the beginning of life.

Elsewhere in the Bible, we read, "Let the weak say I am strong" (Joel 3:10).

Amid this chaos, I went on a business trip to Germany. Their local R&D director, Jean-Michel Anspach, a Belgian who had been my coworker in Brazil, mentioned a vacancy about to open up in his group based in Germany. After I reviewed the ideal background and profile of the job, I said he could sign me up. Having worked for a Swiss, a Mongolian, a German, a Japanese, and a Canadian, I saw this potential move as a good one. I also considered it a good opportunity to brush up on my German. Halfway thorough the negotiations, however, Jean-Michel resigned from the company and I was back to square one. Along with his departure went my opportunity, or so I thought, but God had better plans, which only later would I understand.

I continued living in the fullness of my faith. One weekend, when I was teaching an FGBMFI Evangelistic Seminar in the city Betim–Minas Gerais, one of the attendees came up to me at the end of the seminar. He told me that he had felt it in his heart to pray for me because God had showed him that I was going through a tough time. I had not said anything about the construction loss except to God and my wife, and she did not travel for that seminar. Neither did the hosts have any way of contacting her or knowing about it, unless they had been told by God. I humbly accepted his offer to pray over me, which he did by laying his hands on my head and asking God to give me victory over all the hardships I was facing. In the end, he told me that God would give me a great victory, but that before I saw my victory, God would first take me to a distant land.

About a month later I was again teaching and preaching, this time in the city Cuiabá, Mato Grosso state. God brought a revival to that place that night, and after my preaching, several people came forward asking me to pray for them, which I did. I had taken the opportunity to take a vacation and visit the Pantanal (Floodplains) with my family. When my family and I got back to the apartment where we were staying, some ten people from that church showed up at the door wanting me to pray for them individually. I complied with the requests, and when I was finished, a woman in the group said that I had prayed for everyone but that no one had prayed for me. She then began to lead a prayer over me, and at the end of her intercession, she told me that God would give me a great victory over discrimination, finance, and work-related battles, but that in doing so, He would lead me to a distant land. I believed and accepted her words as a message from God because I had told no one about my situation at work or my financial setback. Campo Grande was about a thousand miles away from Betim and there was absolutely no communication between the two groups. How come the message given to me in Campo Grande have reinforced the message I was given in Betim? It had to be God.

The church I attended in São José dos Campos had a travel choir. One day this choir went to sing at a church in the city of Varginha (MG), and I was the minister designated to accompany them. That evening was a special event and many people had been invited, so the church was filled to capacity with some people standing in the aisles. Pastor Josias Paulino, from the city of Guarulhos-SP, was the guest speaker. The choir presented and I was given the opportunity to address the church by way of introducing the choir.

The preacher started to deliver his message, but after preaching for only a couple of minutes, he stopped and turned in my direction. Then he told me that he had never met me and did not know who

I was, but that he could not proceed with the sermon without first letting me know of a message God was giving him to tell me. He then said, "You are going through a major rejection at work and you have a major financial challenge. God asked me to tell you tonight that he has already prepared your victory. But before you receive your victory, He will move you and your family to a distant country."

The person in Betim had no connection to the person in Cuiaba, who had no knowledge of the person in Varginha. And yet the three messages were identical, so I had no doubt that God was on the move. If God were a human being, I would say to him, as a joke, "What's that all about, God? I tell you my secrets and you make them public?" Thank God he is not one of us but is God the sovereign and holy Lord of hosts, who is keen to reveal what he will do for his loved ones. He is the one who said, "Shall I hide from Abraham what I am about to do?" (Genesis 18:17).

On our way back home from Varginha, I talked to my wife and daughters, and we decided that the way to show God that we believed his messages was for us to start the process of moving. The first thing was to get everyone in the family a passport. We did not know where we would move to, but we knew that we would need passports, something my wife and daughters did not have. In November 1993, the whole family was equipped with passports. We did not apply for the visa, because in addition to not knowing where we were going, it would have to be a work visa, for which I could not apply on my own. I confess that I felt like Abraham when God said to him, "Go from your country, your people and your father's household to the land I will show you" (Genesis 12:1). I find it interesting that Abraham did not know where he was going, but he knew with whom he was going.

In February 1994, I received a call from the US headquarters inviting me to move to Shanghai, China, and lead the development and introduction of a category of products in that country. My job there would also include startup of the company's R&D center in China. I had been mentally prepared to move to Europe, but I was a little shocked to hear about China. I replied that I would need to check the place out, learn more about the scope of work, see the proposed compensation, visit the site, and then discuss the whole plan with my wife and kids.

The company would fully cover visit expenses for my wife and me, but being that far away from the children for a whole week was not acceptable to Celia. Knowing all the prophecies that had come our way, she decided to give up the visit and delegate to me the decision on

Abraham did not know where he was going, but he knew with whom he was going.

the feasibility of making that move. So I went to China with the mission of seeing it through my wife's eyes as well.

My visit to China was anything but thrilling and a dream coming true, but neither was it disappointing. I met with the leaders of Johnson & Johnson in China and heard from them about their R&D needs. They would have loved for me to accept the job on the spot, but even after the visit, I was not yet ready to do that. I told them that I liked the professional challenge, but that I would need yet another two weeks before I could get back to them with an answer. I would first need to share with my wife my impressions of the place, work, and school for the children, and talk with her about how we would live in a place where we did not speak the local language.

When I refused to answer on the spot, I could feel some apprehension and concern that I would turn down the job offer. When asked about my likelihood of accepting the job, I answered it was 50/50, which didn't help to alleviate their concern. I wanted to neither lose bargaining power nor put my

I never show weakness during a negotiation and accept whatever is offered without a chance of negotiating it up.

wife on the spot. But when I said 50/50, I actually meant that I had fully accepted the offer but that I had no clue what my wife would say. Had I jumped to accept their offer right away, though I desperately could have used the extra compensation to build my dream house, I wouldn't have yet heard my family's opinion—and my wife and daughters were more important to me than money. Also, I never show weakness during a

My wife and daughters were more important to me than money.

negotiation and accept whatever is offered without a chance of negotiating it up.

I then returned to Brazil and reported my findings to my wife. We both thought it was the most challenging decision we had ever faced. Celia, the eldest of seven children, faced the prospect of moving to the other side of the world, while all six of her siblings were living within a five-minute drive of her parents.

We weighed the pros and cons, and we spent a significant amount of time in prayer. Because we had received prophetic word that we were temporarily going to a distant country, however, we understood this move to be what God had planned for us. Therefore we decided to pre-accept the offer, with our final decision pending the compensation, which we had not yet seen.

It is always good to go to the negotiating table knowing your value. Upon receiving the salary offer, I decided to run it by my coworker, a British citizen resident in Brazil who had recently returned from a three-year assignment to China. He looked at the compensation I was being offered and said it was good. Because I knew him well, I sensed that, in fact, he wanted to tell me that the offer could be better. So I took a bolder approach and asked him how much a European or an American could be making for doing that same job in China, to which he responded some 30 percent more than I was offered. I thanked him for his openness.

Then I informed USA Human Resources that, for that proposed compensation, I would not accept the job offer. They explained to me all the company policies for international assignments, and in all honesty I never thought the policies seemed unfair. In developing that offer for me, they had followed every detail of the policy for expatriates—home country salary, plus cost-of-living allowance, plus round-trip home for vacation, three weeks of time off outside China but within Asia for rest and relaxation, school for the children, company car and driver, and housing. Nothing was missing, but my issue was that the base for the calculation was my Brazil salary, which was significantly low when compared internationally.

I understood the calculation, but that did not change my opinion that the offer was too low. If they wanted me to take the job, they would have to do something outside of corporate guidelines. To let them know that I had a reference for comparison, I asked them to look at what an American or British citizen was making in China for a job at the same level I was offered. The company had an urgent need for me to be in China because the project kickoff was already scheduled. I had heard that in the past, they had considered sending both a product developer and a process development leader to China. Because of my profile, I could do both jobs, which is what they had offered me with some potential for future advancements elsewhere in the company other than in China.

Rather than convincing me to take the job, however, that was further reason for me *not* to accept it at the compensation offered. I refused to be paid less than one person for doing the jobs of two people. That's how I heard it. I continued to make the point that my compensation needed to be reviewed, even though I was eager to get a salary increase and build my dream house. I told them that I didn't mean to be rude, but that I simply would not take the job for the compensation offered. Finally, after failed attempts to persuade me to accept the proposal as it was, Human Resources took the situation to the vice president who would be my manager.

Resolute and decisive as always, the vice president picked up the phone in New Jersey and called me in Brazil. She told me that she did not disagree with the points I had raised on compensation, and therefore she gave me her word that she would personally take care of making sure I would have fair compensation. She warned me that it could take a few months, though; since it fell outside the company's guidelines, this would need high-level approval. She asked me to trust her and accept the offer, and I didn't view that as a gamble. I did trust her, so I agreed to move to China. I was financially weakened by the loss of a hundred thousand dollars to a bankrupt house builder, but that would not make me lower my value. On the contrary, I like to tell people that I never trade down. It is my

In any negotiation, it is always good to go to the negotiating table knowing your value.

responsibility to negotiate what I think I deserve, and this negotiation is not something I ever consider delegating.

After I told my future manager that I trusted her, my family started packing for the move. My wife and daughters began English classes, but

In my life, I have learned to appreciate people who either help or get out of the way.

with the emotional impact of the move, those lessons at the time did not sink in. In my life I have learned to appreciate people who either help or get out of the way, and I was often reminded of that while preparing to move to China. At the English institute, my wife ran into the Johnson & Johnson Human Resources manager's wife, who told Celia that her husband said that I was crazy and making an insane decision to take my family with me to China. My wife came home with teary eyes to tell me what had happened in her English classroom. Celia had accepted what the HR manager's wife said as absolute truth, even though it originated with a person who only pretended to know more than I did about China.

I reaffirmed that I had thoroughly checked the place out, spoken with another expatriate living in China, and had an open discussion with a family that had just returned to Brazil from China. Then I told her I did not believe that the Human Resources manager had any data to back up his comments about living in Shanghai. As if those points were not enough, I reminded her that we had heard from God about this move. I passed on to my wife a confidence that I never knew I had.

A group of coworkers organized a going-away party for us. Everybody seemed to be having a great time, *until* the wife of one of my coworkers turned to Celia and said that she had a friend who had just returned from China. She said that her friend had a tough time in China because the language was the most difficult in the world. In general, this woman had nothing good to say to my wife about living in China. Again I had to do damage control because someone had

Through faith, we won over everyone who, intentionally or through ignorance, had been opposed to this change.

119

missed the opportunity to remain silent and appear intelligent. Instead, she had chosen to spew garbage and reveal that she was not as smart as we had thought.

The truth is that through faith, we won over everyone who, intentionally or through ignorance, had been opposed to this change. We left for China. My sister, who had lived with us for twelve years, gave up her job and moved with us to the other side of the planet.

17

China through My Eyes

We arrived in Shanghai, China, in late June 1994. For the first seventy-two days, we lodged at a hotel while we waited for the builders to finish the international house complex where we would live. Everything was new for my family and me—the culture, the food, the need to haggle in every purchase, the way people socialize, and the intrinsic curiosity for learning more about the Western part of the world. The hotel was part of a global chain, thus pretty much a little bit of the Western world in China.

I immediately started working, and each day I would learn things that it would have been nice to know beforehand. For example, because it was summer vacation, the families of expatriates living in Shanghai had flown to their home countries and only the people assigned to work in China were still there. Another thing was that there were several vaccines we should have had before moving to China, but no one ever told us about them. Also, had I known I would be living in a hotel for ten weeks with my wife, two children, and sister, I would have planned things differently and staggered their arrival accordingly. The things we should have known beforehand, but didn't, made life more difficult for my family. During the hot and humid summer, they were virtually confined to the hotel and its surroundings, especially since nobody except me spoke anything other than Portuguese, which was useless in Shanghai.

At work I was soon nicknamed BaXiNim (Bā-she-ning), which

121

in the Shanghainese dialect meant *Brazilian*. A few days after my arrival, the Brazil men's soccer team won the FIFA World Cup. That opened doors for getting to know people because every other person who learned I was from Brazil wanted to chat about soccer. As I started getting familiar with my new job, the challenges seemed greater than I had anticipated. A significant part of my work was to identify and develop local suppliers to provide raw materials that met the quality standards set by my company. That required that occasionally I would travel within China. My impression of the Chinese people could not have been better. They were hard workers, intelligent, respectful, and great hosts.

To the best of my recollection, every potential supplier I visited organized either dinner or lunch in the finest restaurant in the area. They would bring along half a dozen members of their staff and reserve a dining room with a karaoke machine in it. Although it always seemed like a time to eat, drink, and be merry, we would engage in serious business conversations. They were always receptive to understanding and learning about changes that would be needed in their processes to comply with J&J standards of quality. Chinese businessmen had awakened to worldwide business opportunities and didn't want to miss an opportunity to have Johnson & Johnson as their customer, because that could be widely viewed as a valuable endorsement to be leveraged.

I was exposed to culinary experiences that I found exotic, though the Chinese didn't see it that way. I'm not very selective about what I eat, but I found myself embarrassed to once have to reject certain delicacies offered by a supplier to me as a guest of honor. A small bamboo basket was placed on the lazy Susan that stopped right in front of me, as I was the first to be served. I looked at it and, already knowing the answer, I asked the purchasing manager what it was. He traveled with me and also served as an interpreter from English into Mandarin. I realized that the basket contained boiled tadpoles, but as he probably did not know how to translate *tadpole* from Mandarin to English, he told me it was a kind of seafood. I told him that I knew it was extremely rude to reject food that was offered to me, but unfortunately I was not in the mood for seafood that night. I think his translation to Mandarin was that I was a vegetarian because that was all that was served me for the rest of the night. Nonetheless, I have to tell you that I enjoyed Chinese cuisine, and still do to this day. I had some of the most delicious food while living in China.

As we were in the habit of regularly attending an evangelical church, we found a Chinese church that provided headphones so that foreigners could follow the simultaneous translation of the sermon from Mandarin to English. We would attend this church in downtown Shanghai, and after we got home from church, I would summarize the sermon for my wife, who at the time did not understand English.

Little by little, expats were returning from vacation and we were forming a new circle of friends. We moved to our fifteen-hundred-square-foot apartment, the girls started classes at the Shanghai American School, and we found an international group of evangelicals who met every Sunday in the ballroom of one of the hotels in Shanghai. Celia started English lessons, and while practicing English with a neighbor, she found out about an International Fellowship Group, a group of evangelical expatriates who, in addition to the Sunday service, also held home fellowship group meetings on weekdays.

At the gated community in which we lived, we got to know people who would become great friends. Among them was the Wittman family, Americans who were also part of the International Evangelical Fellowship in Shanghai. Step by step, I would learn that even when I'm confused, God does not stop his plans for our lives, but brings them to fruition.

Though I had been ordained a pastor in October 1992 for the expatriate evangelical community, initially I did not identify myself as a pastor. I could run any business meeting in English, but preaching in English would require more language skills than I had at the time. There were about half a dozen businessmen who led the group, and four of them took turns preaching, but there was no minister because the Chinese government did not allow ministers into the country.

For the 1995 Chinese New Year, all four preachers would be out of the country, and the group leaders were concerned about not having a service that day. Among those of us planning to attend services on that holiday, I was asked if I would be comfortable delivering the sermon. Preaching was something that I had been doing for about thirty years, but I had never preached in English. Nevertheless, they did not need to know that, so I said, "Sign me up." I accepted the challenge and prepared myself to the best of my ability to deliver the sermon.

In February 1995 I was discovered as a pastor and speaker for that international evangelical community, and from then on, I was one of the regular speakers and also the person responsible for leading Communion. Among evangelicals who attended these meetings were families from various countries, and all continents were represented. There, for the first time, I had a UK ambassador congratulate me and thank me for my sermon. I was working as a part-time missionary funded by Johnson & Johnson, where I worked full-time. We organized several small groups for home Bible study, including one that I hosted and led.

There were twenty-seven thousand foreigners in Shanghai, but there was only one medical doctor who spoke English. In that city of twelve million inhabitants, only two supermarkets sold imported products, which generated price speculation and a rush to buy them as soon as they were displayed on shelves. We used to buy milk from England, cheese from the Netherlands, rice from Thailand, and meat from Australia for twenty dollars per pound.

My personal driver, Mr. Wang, was a necessity, rather than a luxury or premium benefit, and from him I learned a lot about Chinese culture. At first, he did not speak a word of English, and through an interpreter he told me that he would teach me Mandarin. After learning about two hundred words of Mandarin, I told him, via an interpreter, that we would then reverse the strategy and I would teach him English. When I left China, it was very rewarding when my driver told me that thanks to my lessons, he could speak English, which would help him get a better job in China. It makes me feel good when I help someone.

Remember that compensation negotiation I had with the vice president, before leaving for China? At my year-end performance review, I was given the highest rating possible and my base salary was adjusted. No corporate guideline was broken and no exception was granted. But because the plan was to move me to the United States when I left China, I was put on the US payroll, which changed my base salary from a Brazil salary to a US salary, and then assigned to China. My boss had kept her word and honored our agreement, and I would not have expected anything different from a woman of such integrity. In terms of compensation, I was on equal footing with my expatriate peers from developed countries. My work in China was considered exemplary, and I received the highest possible scores on my performance evaluation, which allowed me to recover from the financial loss I had suffered in Brazil when my builder went bankrupt. While I was in China, my brother Dario Junior managed the construction of the house for me, and it was fully built by the end of 1995.

My farewell to China was marked by several tokens of appreciation and a series of dinners with various groups, including the evangelical community, the executive committee of Johnson & Johnson China, the project team I led, and the fifty-two Brazilians living in Shanghai. We heard words that taught us how to appreciate even more the value of sincere friendship and empathy.

The project was complete and my next assignment would be in the United States, where I would join the global leadership of J&J's research, development, and engineering organization. I was first offered a job in R&D, but the project in China had allowed me to leverage my engineering skills like never before. That convinced me that I wanted to pursue a career in R&D engineering, rather than R&D product development. I firmly believed there was more opportunity for me to succeed in that field, and the organization would benefit more from having me there. In engineering I could use my strongest background, which was in manufacturing equipment design. Therefore I was respectfully not flexible in my desire to be in engineering, and a manager position was carved out for me in the

R&D engineering group based in New Jersey. I never felt I was in any position to *demand* the job I wanted, but humbly and decisively I tried to make my point by highlighting gaps in engineering that I could fill. In a sense, I did nothing but take ownership of my career, and to this day I appreciate the people who were kind enough to give me that opportunity.

> *In a sense, I did nothing but take ownership of my career, and to this day I appreciate the people who were kind enough to give me that opportunity.*

18

A Fresh Start

In early November 1995 we landed in New Jersey, just days before what would come to be known as the blizzard of the century. A new beginning was just waiting for us.

It did not take me long to conclude that visiting the United States on business and meeting with co-workers was one thing, but now being based here and competing with them was something else. I lived

Thanks to my reaction to the discrimination I went through in Brazil, I became a resilient person, determined to use and display my fullest potential.

through it, but I'd rather a million times over be in an honest and competitive environment where progress and recognition are based on competence and accomplishments. I had agonized in Brazil about having the color of my skin thrown in as a deterrent to my professional success. Thanks to my reaction to the discrimination I went through in Brazil, I became a resilient person, determined to use and display my fullest potential.

Compared with living in China, living in the United States seemed more like living on another planet. Everything had more ice in it—the water, the tea, and the weather.

In the week we landed in New Jersey, I looked in the Yellow Pages and found a church just a few blocks down the street from our hotel, right across the street from Princeton University. It was the same denomination we used to be part of in Brazil. We were well received there, where we found a young Brazilian lady with an American husband who were keen to make sure we were fine and comfortable in that church. We filled out a visitor's card and checked the box for those looking for a home church. The lead pastor gave us a follow-up call, and as soon as we moved into our house, he paid us a visit.

I had met my coworkers, we had a church to attend, and the girls already were familiar with the American school system, the same system they had attended in China. Everything seemed in motion for a successful transition to the challenges of the developed world. Our American dream was coming true, as we could now go out and actually find exactly the product we wanted at a fair price, with good quality, and as much of it as we wanted. Gasoline was cheaper, and the price of a car was ridiculously low compared with prices in China or Brazil. For the six years I was an expatriate in the USA, among the benefits provided by the company were a company car, housing, and annual home leave. Also the company picked up the tab for income tax in excess of what I would pay in Brazil. We needed two cars, but I finally could afford to drive my new 528 BMW, which I replaced a few years later with a new Mercedes E350 AWD.

After I had worked in the United States for six months, a re-structuring occurred and some people were laid off. In that organizational change, I was promoted to director of engineering with global responsibilities. I was blessed, happy, and grateful to God. Finally my career had taken off in the direction of senior leadership, and while some people were being moved out of the organization, I was fortunate to move up.

One evening we were visited by my former director in Brazil, the man who had told me that because of the color of my skin, I would never rise above the level of manager. He came to the United States on a business trip, and I invited him to dinner at our house. It was a pleasant evening; we talked about a variety of different things because culturally his overall knowledge seemed to be above that of the average person.

As we were enjoying a delicious dinner prepared by my wife, I couldn't help but remember that when he was my boss, I had asked him about the possibility of spending a training period in the United States. His answer at the time was that I should forget that idea because I would never live in the United States through Johnson & Johnson. Ironically I was there now, living in the United States, with Johnson & Johnson, and in a job two levels higher than when we had that conversation about being trained in the USA.

My faith has taught me an important lesson: We have the choice either to believe that we are what people say we are or to believe that we are what God says we are. The option and course of action are totally ours. Though I remembered my former boss's exact words, I did not think of playing them back to him, but I thanked my God for not having given up on me. Moreover, despite hearing words of discouragement, God always ended up bringing my way people with a genuine interest in my advancement and growth, provided I would do my part by delivering on or above business commitments.

Over the years, in my engineering director job, I had a wide range of responsibilities within the R&D global engineering group. Every time I saw before me a new opportunity, that would remind me of the biblical text from Ezekiel that was interpreted to say that I would reach the highest position of an organization.

> *If God promises something but I do not do my part, I am still not going anywhere.*

When God promises things, they happen according to his time, so I did my best to be ready. I do not believe God would give a job to a person who was not qualified to perform. If he promised and I was not qualified, it would come, but it would take some time for me to get ready for that job. The good thing is that he would provide the means for me to be trained and developed for the job he had promised me. If God promises something but I do not do my part, I am still not going anywhere.

When the pastor of my church in Princeton invited me to run for deacon in the church election, I accepted and was elected. Everything was going well, and everyone was reasonably happy with the job I was doing as a deacon. But then

> *We have the choice either to believe that we are what people say we are, or to believe that we are what God says we are.*

one day, someone from Brazil who recently had moved to the United States and was looking for a home church knocked on the church doors on a weekday looking for a Brazilian pastor named Samuel. Later the pastor spoke with me and found out that I was a pastor, although I had been serving as a deacon. I explained to him that my full-time job was with J&J, and as far as the church was concerned, I was there to serve as a volunteer in whatever capacity I was needed.

So that same pastor contacted the regional district of that denomination and introduced me to the presbyter, so that he could take care of the paperwork for me to be recognized in the United States as an ordained pastor. After fulfilling some college-level materials for theological training formerly done in Brazil, I was ordained a pastor in the United States by the Assemblies of God, serving at Nassau Christian Center right across the street from Princeton University.

There, I first had the opportunity to teach Sunday school and lead home fellowship groups. A couple of years later, I was appointed to lead the Sunday school and became the church's associate pastor. Our Sunday church services were in the morning, so sometimes I was invited to preach in a Brazilian church that had evening services. Again, my main activity and occupation was the corporate business of J&J, but whenever possible I was voluntarily serving in the church.

As the associate pastor, I would fill in for the senior pastor in his absence, and sometimes, in addition to the Bible education activities, I would preach at the main service on Sunday morning. One day as I was wrapping up my sermon, I made an altar call for those who had a prayer request. I told them that they didn't need to tell me why they needed prayer, because God, who answers prayers, already knew why they came to the altar.

After I prayed for one woman, she noticed tears in my eyes and began to cry. She was sobbing uncontrollably to see that my eyes were flooded with tears, and she was barely able to speak. But she managed to tell me that in her forty-six years of life, many

I was fulfilling my mission in life of helping people relieve their burden of sorrow and disappointment.

130

people had prayed for her and counseled her, but never, ever, had anyone cried for her—and for that reason, she was crying. She asked for permission to give me a hug, and I knew that lady left the church confident that God loved and cared for her. I continued to see her in church, and I have every reason to believe that God solved whatever problem she was facing that day. I felt that by praying for that woman, I was fulfilling my mission in life of helping people relieve their burden of sorrow and disappointment.

With fluency in English and Portuguese and basic conversation in German and Italian, I learned Spanish pretty much by osmosis while I lived in New Jersey. I bought a Bible in Spanish and started to read it. I also took advantage of making conversation in Spanish when I came across people who spoke it.

In my professional activities, I was happy about having been promoted to global director, and I was pleased to live in New Jersey. But I started to feel uneasy because I had been at that level for several years. I was ready for another promotion, but I had no sign it was in the works. One of the problems many companies face, for which they suffer some consequences, is that they don't tell their employees where they stand in their careers and how they are perceived by the organization. It's only fair for companies to do that, so that their employees can choose to either correct course or keep doing with excellence what they do well. For the company, the consequences of not telling people is that talent ends up being lost to the competition when employees lack transparency and an understanding of their chances for advancement where they are. When companies lack the courage to tell employees the truth, even people who are doing a poor job believe things are going well, and employees can be surprised by an unanticipated layoff. Lack of transparency can also lead to employees with great potential leaving the company because of their personal perceptions that they aren't progressing.

Talent ends up being lost to the competition when employees lack transparency and an understanding of their chances for advancement where they are.

One day a group of directors was invited to attend a breakfast with one of the Johnson & Johnson presidents. I entered the room clueless about why I was there, and I found it strange *Leaders owe honesty to their people.* because normally we were informed of the agenda for any event. The twenty people in the room were asked if anyone knew why we were there. One person said, "Because we are considered directors with high potential for career advancement." That came as a surprise to me because my own immediate leader, the vice president, had never told me I was on the talent list of people with high potential. I learned that as leaders, we need to make our employees aware of their situation with whatever news we have, whether that news is good or not. Leaders owe honesty to their people.

Another lesson I've learned is that if we want something, we need to demonstrate our desire and go after it. In 2003, I was approached by Human Resources to be the director who would analyze the results of an internal survey of the company code of ethics, known internally as "Our Credo." I would do all the analysis and a vice president would present the results to all global R&D vice presidents. In graduate school, I had taken extra statistics classes and even taught statistics at the engineering program of UNIVAP, a local university in São José dos Campos. I am an analytical person, so I gave my best shot at analyzing the global Credo Survey data, comparing it with the previous year's, indicating trends, and spotting gaps and opportunities for leveraging.

With the analysis in hand, I then presented my conclusions to the vice president with whom I was to work on this and her boss, the global head of R&D. Being congratulated for the analysis made me a happy camper, but my excitement was short lived. The next thing I heard was that the VP now had the challenge of digesting my presentation and presenting it to her peers the next day, for joint development of an action plan on corrective actions. I had thought all along that this analysis would provide me the opportunity to be exposed to twenty-two vice presidents, of whom maybe one or two knew me well whereas the others didn't even know I existed. Those people sitting around that table would decide my future in the organization, so I badly wanted to show off for them.

I returned to my office thinking that the decision of that executive vice president, the global head of R&D, was based on my reputation for doing good work behind the scenes for others to present and take the credit. I needed to reverse their perception that I would have problems in leading a group of peers. There would be no better opportunity than this one presented itself because it would allow me to lead a group of people in positions higher than mine.

I called the vice president and told her there were ninety-four slides in the presentation but I thought we needed only about a dozen of them because most were backups I had prepared in case questions arose. I went on to say that although she was more than capable of presenting the data, in my opinion that would be time consuming because it was already 6:00 p.m. For each slide I had a specific message and conclusion in mind, and the meeting would start at nine o'clock the next morning. So I suggested that I present the analysis, and she would then lead the discussion on the action plan. Apparently that sounded like music to her ears because I could hear a sigh of relief, but she needed to run the idea by her boss. She asked me how comfortable I would be presenting to that group, and upon hearing that it would be my dream come true, she called her boss, who agreed with my recommendation. I was up until two o'clock in the morning because I knew that presentation would be my best exposure up to that point in my career. Also the timing and audience seemed to be right on target because later that week they would review the top talent list and promotion recommendations.

The next morning, because of my success and the leadership demonstrated in my presentation and discussion with the vice presidents, I became seen as an invaluable leader. If opportunity does not knock on your door, you go knock on the door of opportunity. Opportunities will never track you down; you need to go after them.

Opportunities will never track you down; you need to go after them.

19

The Buck Stops Here

The company was reorganized once again, and I was now reporting to a vice president who had previously been my peer. Because he knew well my strengths and opportunities for development, he hired a coach, who held a doctorate in psychology, to work with me on a career development plan. Her job was first to identify points for me to develop in relation to the requirements for the next level of career advancement and then address how I could bridge the gap.

After consulting senior executives with whom I interacted on a regular basis, her conclusion was that I always had great ideas, but that in leadership meetings I was too quiet. I would step up and say something only when asked directly; I was not effective in influencing group discussion because I participated only when stimulated by a direct question. Now I had the truth said to my face, and I had the choice to either do something about it or forever stay put.

Now I had the truth said to my face, and I had the choice to either do something about it or forever stay put.

Three independent sectors make up J&J. My interpretation of my coach's findings was that I wouldn't be promoted within the consumer sector, where I was already labeled as a noninfluential leader. However, I assumed that having been labeled a quiet leader would not be an impediment to my advancement in the medical devices or pharmaceutical sectors because in interviews there I would not come across as a quiet person. With that in mind, I applied for senior director jobs in both the pharmaceutical and medical devices sectors of Johnson & Johnson.

When I was in the final stages of the selection process for these other sectors, a peer of mine who was a senior director moved to another area, and I was consulted about my interest in filling that vacant position. It was explained to me that if I accepted that job, they would expand it. The packaging equipment group, part of my job at the time, would go with me to the other group. I felt pretty good about my chances for a promotion there, since the job of a senior director was being expanded and offered to me. To my surprise, however, I was told that it would be a lateral move and I wouldn't be promoted to senior director.

Upon hearing that news, I did not feel I was in any position to negotiate up; they knew I was a forthcoming person in any situation. I did, however, tell them about the vacancies that I had bid on in the other two sectors. As I explained to them, I needed a job, and if this lateral move in the consumer sector was the job in which they wanted me, I would take it. But if one of the other sectors called to offer me a senior director position, I would accept in a heartbeat. After my vice president and his boss talked it over, I was promoted to senior director.

Some people like to complain and blame others, but my experience tells me that I should never accept something with which I disagree without first making my case. The title of my predecessor had been senior director, and the job I was offered had an even broader scope, so a lateral move did not seem right. I had voiced my feelings about that to the appropriate person, who, by the way, was one of the most reasonable people I have ever met.

I was now a person with greater responsibilities, leading an excellent team of highly competent professionals, with people based in North America, South America, Europe, and Asia. So it was not unusual for me to travel internationally for business meetings.

With every change for the better and professional advancement that came my way, I would go back to my Bible and read Ezekiel

17:23–24. As I read those verses, I was reminded of the interpretation of what they meant for my career and how God would continually bless my life. I became a senior director and built a good reputation at that level, and occasionally peers would seek me out for words of advice.

I was aware that vice president vacancies were scarce and extremely competitive, but I also believed God's promise that I would make it to that level. Therefore I continued to do the best job I could and strive to progress. One lesson life taught me is that in order to make something happen, we first need to believe it is achievable and then make every effort to get there. If I have a promise, but I become hesitant and doubt that it will happen, I won't put my best foot forward—and as a result, it will not happen.

> *One lesson life taught me is that in order to make something happen, we first need to believe it is achievable and then make every effort to get there.*

Several times throughout my career, I felt I had been passed over for promotions, even though I recognized the merit of people who were promoted ahead of me. I always tried to understand which job requirements I had come up short on, and how the colleagues promoted met or exceeded those same requirements. By understanding that gap, I could prepare myself for the next wave of promotions.

I cannot say I was joyful about the promotion of someone whom I considered less prepared than myself. But when I felt dejection, it was like a bird flying over my head, rather than one that made its nest there. If I had used my energy anguishing and feeling embittered about the success of other people, I would have missed out on the opportunity to work on my own development and advancement. After all, I always believed that

> *I always believed that my success would be built on continuous improvement. In other words, I have to be better tomorrow than I am today.*

> *When I felt dejection, it was like a bird flying over my head, rather than one that made its nest there.*

my success would be built on continuous improvement. In other words, I have to be better tomorrow than I am today.

The skills and prerequisites for certain jobs would change more frequently than you would think. In fact, sometimes I felt like requirements changed only because each successive leader had his or her own preferences. That meant that even though I would

We live in a world where people seem to be ashamed to admit that they do not know something.

prepare intensely for a job, so that I was able to meet every requirement, suddenly a different hiring manager with a completely different set of requirements could come into play. Therefore the people who show flexibility, openness to change, and a determination to never stop learning are those who progress.

We live in a world where people seem to be ashamed to say that they do not know something. Today, instead of just admitting that "I do not know," people say that they will use a search engine to find the answer. No one expects you to know everything, but you will always be highly regarded if you know *who* knows the answer and are able to connect with that person for help. I do not necessarily consider myself a professional expert on anything, but I have always tried to find out who had the answer for what I did not know. In a nutshell, my advice is that you don't try to know everything, but instead that you always try to find the most appropriate person to help you out in any given situation. That's interdependence.

Another fact that made a difference in my career was that from the moment I handed control of my life over to God, he managed everything infinitely better than I could ever have done. That was a continu-

If you didn't trust the driver, would you take the passenger seat for a long ride?

ous, irreversible, and long-term decision. If you didn't trust the driver, would you take the passenger seat for a long ride?

I was still living in New Jersey, in my senior director of engineering global role, and I remained optimistic about my career advancement opportunities. At times, however, retirement age seemed to be approaching faster than my target job. Suddenly, I was sent to a weeklong training in New Brunswick, New Jersey. The Office of Diversity and Inclusion was offering a training program to forty people at the director and senior director levels from the entire US Johnson & Johnson. This program was called "Crossing the Finish Line," and the participants were all identified as minorities or, to be precise, men of color (yellow, brown, and black). We were African-Americans, Africans, Asians, and Latinos. It was one of the best trainings I ever received.

During the training, I kept thinking that I was stuck in my career. I had been a senior director for more than four years, and I saw no prospect for advancement. Since vice president positions were not posted for people to bid on them, but rather were filled through either succession planning or external hiring, I had not internally applied for any VP job. Then my positive attitude kicked in, and I thanked God for providing me with the opportunity to go through that training, whatever it would be, because its title and scope led me to believe it had to be good.

Part of the training was to sit down and talk with a career coach, and I had the privilege of talking with a retiree from Johnson & Johnson who already knew me. Upon hearing my concern about the lack of opportunity for advancement to vice *Sometimes we do see problems where none exist.* president, he said that my problem was easier to fix than I thought. And he was right because sometimes we do see problems where none exist. He pointed out to me that my career had always progressed in collaboration with a sponsor who knew me well. My sponsors had either created or known about opportunities for my professional growth and promotion, and that strategy had worked well. But now I had caught up in job level with my sponsors, and they were not the hiring managers for the VP positions I wanted. Therefore I should establish lines of contact with the senior leaders who were hiring the vice presidents. He did not use these words, but my takeaway was that I had been barking up the wrong tree. So I changed tactics—and within three months I was being interviewed for vice president positions. We all need someone who has the courage to tell us what we are doing wrong and, if possible, can show us the consequences of our actions. That is the best help we will ever get.

In succession planning, I was now listed as the first person in line to succeed the global vice president of engineering. From one moment to the next, that vice president moved to another sector and the position was open. I approached the hiring manager to make sure I was being considered. During the selection process, reorganization occurred,

Someone who has the courage to tell us what we are doing wrong and, if possible, can show us the consequences of our actions. That is the best help we will ever get.

and the position for which I had spent several years preparing myself was eliminated rather than backfilled.

My opportunity would now have to be found somewhere else in the organization, so I mapped out all possible VP positions for which I considered myself a good fit. In my efforts to gain exposure to those who managed and hired vice presidents, I spoke with presidents and senior vice presidents about my interest in a VP job. But the next opportunity that arose was a lateral move to senior director of supply chain (planning, procurement, manufacturing, and logistics/distribution). Fortunately for me, my new role as senior director of supply chain helped me to develop new skills that made me a stronger candidate for vice president positions.

In early 2011 I applied for the position of vice president of research and development for Latin America—and I was selected for the job. That was the highest R&D office in Latin America, a position reporting to a global organization, and my group included R&D professionals from several countries, such as Ukraine, Poland, Brazil, Mexico,

I had the choice to believe the words of discouragement and limitation that men said to me, or the words of encouragement and promise that God had for me.

Argentina, Colombia, Peru, Uruguay, and Venezuela. The organizational chart seemed to capture the interpretation of Ezekiel 17:23–24 that I had come across during a critical time in my career. I had reached the number one position in an organization that in the past had considered firing me.

Moreover, it was the organization in which two different bosses had warned me that because of the color of my skin, I would never be promoted above the lower level at which I was working at the time. To put things into perspective, my VP position was seven levels above the level that I had been told would be my limit because of the color of my skin. Earlier I mentioned that discrimination taught me to have selective hearing, and this is what I meant. I had the choice to believe the words of discouragement and limitation that men said to me, or the words of encouragement and promise that God had for me. I chose God's words—the obvious choice—because I knew that he would never let me down.

As vice president of research for Latin America, I would lead a group of people who were highly qualified both academically and in terms of creativity and innovation. It was an organization that included people with master's degrees and doctorates, medical doctors, dentists, engineers, pharmacists, chemists, and biologists, to name only a few. These people were so bright that sometimes they made my job look easy.

We won several professional challenges. During my tenure as vice president of R&D, we were assigned to globally manage two categories of consumer products from Brazil. Such opportunities made the team feel recognized, and they strove for even greater innovation because they understood that senior leadership endorsed the things that we were doing well. The R&D center under my leadership was sought after by the media to showcase R&D in Brazil. We had to turn down a few requests for interviews because they were definitely coming in faster than we could handle.

The National Confederation of Industry set up a committee with CEOs of the top forty companies in Brazil, aiming at the development and support of a robust innovation policy for the federal government. Though I was not a CEO, my role of chief innovation officer for Latin America made me the natural J&J representative on this executive committee for innovation. Through my service on this committee, I gained exposure to a highly select group of executives in Brazil, including government officials, ambassadors, and the media. I was invited as a guest speaker to several events organized by the government and trade associations—usually to talk about innovation, but occasionally also to talk about diversity and inclusion.

One of the best TV journalists in Brazil interviewed me at a diversity conference in Sao Paulo. Another journalist, from Brazil's largest TV network, who interviewed me at an innovation seminar in Rio de Janeiro, remarked on how surprised he was at everything my organization had achieved. A multipage article in one of the most respected technical magazines in Brazil depicted the Johnson & Johnson Latin America R&D Center under my leadership as what they called Worldwide Reference.

The exposure was a boost to our morale, though we never felt we needed it, but every instance of recognition also created higher expectations. The US consul invited me to a seminar the consulate was hosting, to speak about the minority leadership role in Brazil. All of this exposure happened because I had a competent team who would always innovate above expectations.

I was most comfortable when speaking about innovation, diversity, and career development, which surprised people who expected technical leaders, such as myself, to be quiet or to engage exclusively in technical talk. I had experienced my share of that, but that was behind me now. In fact, now I had to learn how *not* to monopolize a conversation.

Internally I organized training sessions during which I would pass down to coworkers the lessons I had learned both in the classroom and on the job. I welcomed the opportunity to sit down one-on-one with employees, ranging from lab equipment operators to senior directors. I started doing that because I realized how wonderful it would have been if a senior person had shown me the way at the beginning of my career. Because I did not have that opportunity when I was younger, I decided to do unto others what I had missed.

I hoped that when these people were in leadership positions, they would consider adopting the same practice of trickling down whatever lessons they would feel helpful and worth sharing. I decided to lead and influence by example. I would treat and advise the youngsters as if they were my own sons or daughters. As James tells us, "If anyone, then, knows the good they ought to do and doesn't do it, it is sin for them" (James 4:17).

I decided to lead and influence by example.

20

Stories Worth Sharing

In May 2013, for the first time ever, the CEO of Johnson & Johnson toured the Research & Development Center in the city of São José dos Campos, Brazil. As the Latin America R&D leader, for an hour I had the opportunity to host the top leader of a company employing about 130,000 people.

While the focus of our conversation was innovation, the CEO had a genuine interest in knowing details about the people he was meeting. When in the hallway I mentioned that I had been with the company for thirty-eight years, and that I had worked in Asia, North America, and Latin America, he congratulated me and said he would like to know more about my story.

A coworker once told me that golden opportunities pass by only once in a lifetime, and therefore we should not hesitate to jump out and grab them. In July 2014 I was at the airport in Nashville, Tennessee, waiting to board a plane to Newark, New Jersey. As the flight was delayed by two hours, I grabbed my smartphone and started writing an e-mail to the J&J CEO. Communicating with him was my golden opportunity that would come only once, and I could not miss it. In the e-mail, I mentioned his voiced interest in knowing more about my story. Having never written to the CEO, I pondered that my message had to be meaningful, accurate, and short. I wanted him to read it through and not feel like it was a complete waste of his time. This CEO is not a person who says things just for the sake of saying something. He means what he says; therefore, if he said he wanted to know more about my story, he meant it.

With a little apprehension, I hit Send and off went a one-page summary of this book. It was a challenge to condense it down to one page. I couldn't have done it without remembering the story a friend told me about the student who was asked to write a one-page essay in fifteen minutes. When time was up, the student turned in a three-page essay to the teacher, who reminded him the requirement was for one page. The student turned back to the teacher and said that a shorter version takes longer to write.

I sent the e-mail and boarded the plane for that two-hour flight to New Jersey. Upon arrival, I found the CEO's response with some of the nicest compliments I've ever received, words of thankfulness for the e-mail, and a request for me to schedule some one-on-one time with him whenever I happened to be in the United States because he wanted to hear more about my story. Well, I was in the United States that same week, and for the first time I had an exclusive audience with the most important person in the Johnson & Johnson companies in the world. It was a conversation that has enriched me as a leader, and it made me think a lot about the vision and humbleness of that great leader.

Ten days later, the CEO's blog, which was available to the more than 120,000 employees of Johnson & Johnson, published the story of Samuel Santos. I received hundreds of e-mails, some from people who knew me and some from people about whom I knew nothing. This was the highest visibility my story had before this book. Some people reported that they had read my story to their children; a member of the company's executive committee wrote to me that he choked up when reading my story. Upon receiving all these e-mails, I knew that I had made it this far only because God had blessed me through his infinite love, grace, and mercy.

During the sixteen years I worked at Johnson &

Compared with other countries where I had worked, I felt the United States was a more competitive environment in which people competed based on merit, rather than on skin color.

Johnson in the United States, I never felt even the slightest hint of discrimination. Compared with other countries where I had worked, I felt the United States was a more competitive environment in which people competed based on merit, rather than on skin color. Beyond work and church, I had exposure that reinforced my feeling that I was fitting in gracefully, especially when I was invited by the dean of the School of Arts and Sciences at New York University to talk to parents of newly admitted students. At that same university, a student group invited me to talk about diversity, and one of the top five universities in the country invited me to participate in the design of a training program on supply chain.

My return to Brazil for the vice president job, after seventeen years overseas, was exciting because I was eager to see the significant progress and planned growth. However, life seems to throw me a curveball every now and then, and this time it was a huge one. Within my first month back in Brazil, my dear father, who had been battling Alzheimer's disease for three years, was taken from this life to another.

On that Friday night of June 2011, I drove with my daughter Erika, who was temporarily living in Brazil for an MBA internship, the 280 miles to my parents' home. We planned to visit my father on Saturday morning in the hospital. Just as I was about to leave the house for the hospital, the phone rang. It was my nephew Gilles, who broke the news to me that my father had passed away. I then had the hard task of informing my mother. The sadness that hit me that day is something I can't quite put into words. There was not even time to mourn because by local laws he was to be buried the next day. I had to rush to take care of arrangements for his memorial service, funeral, and burial, something I had never done before. I had no idea whom in the city to contact.

My father was a simple man who came from a peasant life and became a public servant. But throughout his life, he achieved things that he had never dreamed of, such as flying the ten-thousand-mile round-trip to visit with my family in New Jersey between 1998 and 2009, preach the gospel in the United States, and see all of his children being blessed by the God he loved. He traveled several times to the United States to visit with us, and my family was always excited to have him around. We couldn't stop laughing when my father was around because he was such a joyous person. My father was never lonely, but he always liked to participate in all kinds of games, and my daughters loved having him around. He lived here on earth for just shy of eighty-three years, but he was always jovial and young in spirit. I loved him so dearly.

I delivered this eulogy at my father's funeral:

> Ladies and gentlemen, today my hero's life here on earth has ended. With his departure, Heaven is richer and Earth is poorer. The man of whom I had the privilege of being his son and from whom I have learnt many good things that I will carry with me for the rest of my life, Dario dos Santos, was not a perfect man, but the only perfect man who ever walked on Earth was nailed to a cross. My father loved God with all his heart so much that he would serve God and preach the gospel up until Alzheimer's limited him. He would bring people face-to-face with God. I see here the church deacon Luis, who last month I witnessed ministering to my father what only God knew at the time would be his last Communion. Luis, what a privilege you had of doing that for this great, great godly man.
>
> My friends, you have all lost a brother in Christ, a friend, a neighbor, but I have lost my father. My daughters have lost a playful grandfather, and my mother has lost her husband. As I saw his health slowly vanishing away, I mentally prepared myself to live fatherless, or so I thought, but the pain that now makes me sob, choke, and cry to the point that you all see I can barely speak, is the kind of suffering I wish no one would have to face. Though I will miss

the warmth of his embrace, his jokes, and him at the table playing some games and always ready to learn new ones, I can do without all that, but I am not sure how I will be able to move on without relying on his daily prayers on my behalf.

A few minutes ago we heard my brother Dario Junior say that the many prayers for my father to be healed have been answered because in Revelation 21:4 the Bible says that in the city my dad has moved to, "there will be no more death or mourning or crying or pain, for the old order of things has passed away."

My father did not die; he just changed his home address. Considering his financial and academic limitations, he was without a doubt the greatest godly man I ever met. Few people would have the courage he had; no one encouraged me more than this man did, and I regret that he has left this life before I could repay him for some of what he has done for me. Thank you, my beloved father, and until that day when we will be together again, I will miss you, Daddy.

In 2011 when I took over the job of vice president of research and development for Latin America, my continued success in my professional career was still ahead of me to be conquered. But because faith has never taken a backseat with me, it was equally important to find a home church and continue to serve God and his people. I joined the fastest-growing church in São José dos Campos, which had a visionary and tireless pastor. This church grew exponentially and there came the opportunity not only to serve, but also to meet some people and make new friends.

The year after my father's death, my mother came to live with Dario Junior and his family in São José dos Campos. I now had the privilege of spending good quality time with her, and we all rejoiced in being close to her. We made some trips together, and she was always grateful to God for everything.

If I were going to preach, she always wanted to be in the audience, and it was no different regarding my brother Dario Junior. If my nephew Filipe, Silas's son, was the preacher, she would be in attendance as well. She was an unconditional supporter of her descendants. My mother had been through a lot of suffering and pain in her life up to her fifties, but she was nevertheless always cheerful. In late July 2013, she suffered a stroke and spent a week in a coma. Two months shy of her eighty-fifth birthday, she was called home to be with Jesus. Her death was devastating news to me.

Again I was taking care of the preparations for memorial services, funeral arrangements, and burial. This time around, when they broke the news to me, the doctors handed me a prescription for a controlled substance pill that I was to take so that I could handle the bad news. And believe me, I needed it. Otherwise I could not have borne the pain of such a loss.

My daughter Erika, my mother's first grandchild, delivered this eulogy:

> My grandmother grew up in a society where people like her were not seen with good eyes. Her economic conditions, lack of academic background, and the color of her skin precluded her from many opportunities in this life, but she trusted in what she had. She trusted in something that really could change everything; she trusted the Lord her God. She survived with what little she had, worked simultaneously in several jobs, and often grew the family's own food. Despite all the adversities, she was able to raise five children who have become the fruit of hard work and the faith found in her and in my late grandfather Dario. She and my grandfather raised children who became adults of integrity committed to their family and to God. I know she could not be more

proud of each of you and the person each of you has become, the children you were to her, the way you love God, and your families. My grandmother was a person committed to her work and her church, but she had a lot of strong opinions on things. Anyone who knew her can testify that she was not the person to sit down and be quiet, but a person who would always express her opinion. However, she had a very generous heart. She apologized for any little thing with a gesture, such as making delightful food.

She was a person equipped with genuine love who always tried to take care of us all. And to our happiness, it was often through her cooking, a talent that she used not only for her family but also for her church. Several of the best memories of my life were in the kitchen of my grandmother. There we'd laugh for hours while she and my grandfather made bread, huge biscuits, and milk paste. In that kitchen my grandfather told his jokes that had us laughing a lot, not necessarily for the punch line, but usually for his funny way of telling it. I hope he never found out the reason we laughed at his jokes. My grandmother made the best lasagna in the world. When we'd go to her house, everyone already knew: "prepare the oven because we will have lasagna." I remember one day I was paying close attention to how she made the lasagna and asked for the recipe, especially the white sauce, to which she answered a little of this, a pinch of it here, and a handful of this here. So it was hard to get it right. To this day I do not know if she wanted to give away that recipe or keep it to herself because she wouldn't want any competition to her lasagna.

My grandmother always took good care of us. When a grandchild was born, she would come over

and take care of both mother and baby, and sometimes my grandfather came along. From the time I
was born until the time of her death, I know that one
way or another; she took good care of me. I know
that every day she prayed for me. She did not attend
school for a long time but she was a very smart person, and this was my favorite part of it, her way of
being. It's hard to describe, but she had certain sar-
casm and a contagious mood. I can now see much
of it in some of us, her grandchildren.

For as long as I breathe, I will miss her, and I
will love her forever. I know I'm an adult, a married
woman, but to me, still there was no place like my
grandma's lap, her love and wisdom, and all the
good things she learned in the school of life. For
five years I had a very great privilege of being her
only grandchild. With the grace of God I know that
all will go on, but everything will be a little harder
without her. And the great moments of my life will
not be exactly the same because of her absence.

It is very difficult to try to describe in a eulogy
the life of my grandmother, because no matter how
well I do it, it still wouldn't do justice to who she
was. Sometimes the most sober moment in one's
life is when you face the death of a beloved one. On
a day-to-day basis we spend life busy with things we
need to get done, but in moments like this one, we
stop and see that life is like a breath. She was fortunate to live for almost eighty-five years. She was so
strong that I really thought she was going to live to
be one hundred years old. That's life; we go through
this difficult time believing that one day it all will
make sense. Now we just have questions for which
there are no answers but I believe that one day it will
all make sense.

My grandmother read the entire Bible every year. Even a couple of months ago though she was hospitalized and had difficulties in reading, she read her Bible. To end my tribute to her, I share with you that which was the last Bible reading she made on July 25, 2013, which was the thirty-fourth chapter of Psalms: "I will bless the Lord at all times; his praise shall continually be in my mouth. My soul shall make her boast in the Lord."

My pastor also delivered a eulogy that brought much comfort to our hearts. As of August 1, 2013, I was officially an orphan. The two people who had prayed the most for me were my parents, but now they are no longer here among us. I thanked God for the parents I had and pulled myself together as much as I could because I trust God's promises that one day I will see them again.

21

The Legacy

Both of my daughters successfully graduated from one of the best universities in the United States. They continued and advanced in their studies beyond college, and I am grateful to God for the two wonderful daughters he gave me. Though fluent in Portuguese, English is their first language, *When God wants to give you something, the devil is not consulted.* and are both working in marketing and progressing well, to the point that I learn from them. I see in each of them a much better-looking, more talented, younger version of me, and I thank God for their faithfulness to him and their success in their careers. Erika got married in 2005 and Renate in 2010. I have always believed that the blessings from God upon my life were extended to my offspring, and for these children I continually pray. Let me tell you something— when God wants to give you something, the devil is not consulted. So seize everything that God has for your life.

In early 2012 I was vacationing in the United States, and I sat down to talk with Erika about how things were going with her MBA. During the conversation I noticed her teary eyes, and when I asked what was wrong, she almost choked up. She told me that she believed she was sterile because she hadn't been able to get pregnant. I prayed with her and for her, and I told her that God's blessings were for my future generations and that in 2015, she would beget a child. Only her parents and in-laws were informed of her situation, and we were all praying for her to have a baby.

Erika continued her medical appointments and took all possible treatments, but to no avail. Then medical exams indicated that she had some apparent impediments, which could be corrected via surgery. The surgery was scheduled for October 2013, but it would be preceded by a pregnancy test. The pregnancy test came back positive, so Erika did not go through that surgery. Instead, she returned home with the news that she was expecting a baby.

In July 2014, my daughter Erika gave birth to a healthy, handsome boy who was named Samuel. His name meant what had happened—God had answered their prayers.

Among the many things my mother had hoped to see in life was her first great-grandchild, so we never told her that Erika had been facing difficulties in getting pregnant. My mother passed away in August, and in September Erika got pregnant.

In June 2015 my daughter Renate and her husband, David, received the gift from God of the most healthy and beautiful girl I had ever seen, whom they named Elizabeth. Throughout her pregnancy Renate faced a number of challenges and risks. The fetus was diagnosed as underdeveloped and at high risk of being born with a genetic abnormality. For my daughter, that was an emotional roller coaster.

For several years, Renate had had the comfort of knowing that her grandfather prayed for her every day. Now that he was gone, she charged me with that responsibility, and those were big shoes to fill. I agreed and planned that whenever I'd pray, I would include her and the unborn child in my petitions. However, Renate is just as anxious as my mother was, and she wanted me to pray along with her every day. She decided that every night, Celia and I would pray with her and her husband in a videoconference call. We did this for a few weeks while I was in Brazil and they were in Texas. One day, after we prayed, I turned to my wife and told her that after that night's prayer, I had felt a great peace. I had a feeling, whether from God or from myself, that Renate would have a baby girl and the child would have no abnormality.

Two weeks later, Renate and David consulted with the medical specialist in genetic abnormality to whom they had been referred. The doctor looked at the test results and confirmed that she had been pregnant for seventeen weeks. But then he noticed that the calculation had been done at the lab as if Renate had been twenty-one weeks pregnant, which would have distorted the test results. A seventeen-week fetus had been tested and compared against the expected results for a twenty-one-week fetus. The conclusion was that the results indicating genetic abnormality were inconclusive, and that the lab would have to recalculate the results based on the correct age of the fetus. It was a test of faith, but above all an experience that further taught us to approach God and trust him even more.

I continued my job activities in Brazil and started making my plans to return to the United States and retire. The vast majority of people with whom I worked expressed sadness when I spoke about retiring—well, at least my friends did. On the other hand, I saw sadness in my daughters and wife when we talked about staying a little longer in Brazil. Between family and work, the choice was not difficult. My wife and I would return to the United States and join our daughters, grandchildren, and sons-in-law who awaited us here, since they had not moved to Brazil in 2011.

Today I feel comfortable and recognized wherever I go, and I have been to places I never thought I would be invited to. I have come to the conclusion that the poor suffer the greatest discrimination. Growing up, I used to be called poor, black, and Protestant, but now they call me by my titles and in a respectful way. The truth is that I am who I always was. The only thing that changed was my lifestyle because with professional development came an income that allowed me to live differently. Yes, it is a fact that many people will accept you based on your net worth or your influence, rather than on your character and moral values. I decided to cling to God because he made me and accepts me just as I am.

If I have defects or flaws, God knows how to fix them, although

I don't believe he makes faulty people. God does nothing defective. People call other people disabled, but God made everyone. In God's eyes, no one is disabled and everyone is equally important. If some people have physical limitations, compared with whatever standards we set, that's just God giving the rest of us an opportunity to exercise altruism and help them out.

In December 2014 I began to plan my retirement. I requested pension calculations for retirement either in March or September 2016, as I planned on setting money aside to build an orphanage in Haiti. In May 2015 I signed the contract to build a house in Tennessee, where I planned to live as a retiree. The house would be ready in November 2015, and in conversation with management, it was agreed that I would leave the company in December 2015, one day after completing my forty years of service with Johnson & Johnson. That financial proposal was just as good as the others I had considered.

On July 30, 2015, when the announcement of my retirement was posted, a myriad of e-mails arrived with messages that deeply touched my heart. Some were so meaningful that I asked the sender's permission to anonymously include them in this book. E-mails and video messages came from throughout the J&J hierarchy, from people at the lowest levels right up to the CEO. Each one touched me greatly because it reflected how these people had interacted with me and what I meant to them. I had a feeling of mission accomplished— my mission having been to make a positive contribution to the life of every person whom I happened to meet.

My management announced my retirement this way:

> Samuel Santos, Vice President Latin America R&D and product deployment, has informed me of his decision to retire on December 23, 2015, an impressive mark of 40 years with our company.
>
> Sam first joined J&J as a draftsman and progressed through roles of increased responsibilities in the areas of Engineering, Supply Chain, and

R&D. His key accomplishments include working in three continents, creating the Technology Transfer organization concept, developing several products relevant to our Feminine Care business, pioneering the J&J Consumer R&D activities in China, leading Global Engineering, the development and implementation of state-of-the-art production lines, and enabling the launch of new products at competitive costs. In Supply Chain, he led the project of consolidating our Caribbean business into North America, significantly improving our business results in that region; and more recently, he led and coordinated the R&D activities in Latin America, expanding capabilities, implementing new products, and developing a strong and focused organization.

Sam will be greatly missed as an inspirational communicator, a mentor, and a person committed to developing people.

As we prepare to bid him farewell, I want to thank Sam for his dedication to J&J and ask you to join me in wishing him all the best with his plans to dedicate his time to charity, to his church, and to his family, which includes the recent addition of two grandchildren.

Sam is helping ensure a smooth transition with his successor.

He and his wife, Celia, plan on returning to the United States and residing in Nashville, TN.

Included here are two of the many messages I received when the above announcement was posted. The first I also posted in Spanish, the original language in which it was sent:

Apreciado Samuel, no puedo estar mas de acuerdo con las palabras de su jefe sobre lo que has significado para las personas que hemos tenido el placer de conocerte y escucharte. Tu carrera profesional ha sido muy sólida, contribuyendo de forma extraordinaria al negocio, pero pienso que te recordaremos más por inspirador.

Tu me has marcado fuertemente con su entusiasmo y liderazgo ... el Town Hall del año pasado, dejó una huella profunda en mi y me ha permitido este año a mi equipo local, no sólo en mi departamento sino también el de Mexico alcanzando al área técnica de la planta, compartiéndoles la visión de "Todos vamos en el mismo barco" sin importar el área todos hacemos la diferencia, traemos innovación y la venta.

Me alegro mucho de haberte conocido, de haber tenido oportunidad de conversar contigo, de verme influenciada por tu muy personal estilo de liderazgo, motivador y desarrollador de lideres inspiracionales.

GRACIAS! Por todo tu legado. GRACIAS! Por tu sencillez y cercanía. GRACIAS! Por hacer una diferencia. Por seguro te extrañaré, pero también estoy muy segura que tus palabras seguirán acompañándome en mi vida diaria y al momento de tomar decisiones y buscar desarrollar la gente, y muy importante me seguirán ayudando a crecer como persona.

Te deseo lo mejor de la vida en compañía de tu familia y tus nuevos nietos. Sinceramente y con un profundo respeto y cariño.

Translation: Dear Samuel, I cannot agree more with the words of your boss on what you have meant for people who have had the pleasure to meet you and hear you. Your career has been very strong, contributing dramatically to the business, but I think you will be best remembered as an inspirer.

You have marked me strongly with your enthusiasm and leadership ... Last year's Town Hall left a deep impression on me and allowed me to this year with my local team, not only in my department but also of Mexico, reach the plant technical area, sharing the vision "we're all going in the same boat"; regardless of the area we all make a difference, we bring innovation and sales.

I'm glad to have met you, and to have had the opportunity to talk with you, to see myself very influenced by your personal leadership style, motivating and developing inspirational leaders.

THANK YOU! For all of your legacy. THANK YOU! For your simplicity and closeness. THANK YOU! For making the difference. For sure I will miss you, but I'm also pretty sure your words will accompany me in my daily life and when making decisions and seeking to develop people, and they are very important to continue to help me grow as a person.

I wish you the best of life in the company of your family and your new grandchildren. Sincerely and with deep respect and affection.

Another director sent me this message in e-mail:

Sam, it's hard to write a farewell message to someone who was my "conscience" for so long. You surely were a very inspirational leader for me, and to know your story either through the CEO's blog or through your lectures at corporate training for directors made me reflect even more about the unique person you are. I'm sure you are very proud of your story and believe you can be even more proud to bring your forty-year career with Johnson & Johnson to a close on a high note, leaving a legacy of having made an outstanding transformation in the Latin America Research & Development Center. Your coaching either by complimenting, critiquing, or by offering words of wisdom will forever be treasured because your words were fundamental in shaping me up as a corporate leader and as a human being. Many of the things you passed on to me I plan on cascading down to others, especially to the youngsters in this organization. I will really miss you as a leader, but more so as the friend who in recent years has always been there for me. Warmest regards.

At Johnson & Johnson Brazil, there was a huge retirement ceremony. Not even in my wildest dreams had I imagined such a wonderful farewell, which I definitely did not feel I had done anything to deserve. Hundreds of people were in attendance, as well as a musical band playing my favorite songs, I was asked to plant a tree and I was given several tokens of appreciation, including a video message from the Johnson & Johnson CEO and other senior executives in the company. People showed gratitude and affection beyond what I could have imagined. If I was the leader they claimed me to have been, that was only because my ethical principles of leading others demanded that I treat everyone as I would like to be treated. I got that from the Bible, which says, "Do unto others as you would have them do to you." The Bible gave me the confidence to be that kind of leader, just because it was the right thing to do. I always tried not to think of recognition because that would defeat the purpose of serving others, but rather to maintain a selfless attitude. People come to work every day expecting their leaders to be fair, ethical, and responsible. I did my best to make my actions reflect that, and if I failed anyone, it was not from malice or a hidden agenda, but only because their expectation was eventually beyond my reach.

I said these words in return:

In my most daring imagination, I never glimpsed a farewell like this. It reflected what we were to each other in the professional interaction that we had for a period of time that varied from person to person.

In the embrace, the kiss on the face, the handshake, the message written or spoken, in the high-five, you have reached my heart and marked my story. In these four and a half years I've held this position, I've met many professionals whom I learned to admire for their qualities, skills, and character. You made my job look easy, and because we had people of such caliber, we occupied a prominent place in the worldwide R&D organization of our company. We presented to the highest executives of the corporation, showed up in the media, and were approached by embassies as a reference, and all this was due to your merit,. If it were not for you, I would not have our accomplishments to showcase. Here I've learned a lot from some whom forever I will call my professors.

In this forty-year journey I relied on people who equipped me for battle, others who were my shield when I was under attack, and those who pledged empathy and joint efforts so we could win battles and wars as a group. Many of you supported me anonymously and never told me about it, but via other channels I knew of your support and this makes me admire you even more. This journey here from draftsman to vice president shows the greatness of this company and the reality of opportunities.

Three people have been very important in my career. One of them discovered me and supported me in a career transition phase in 1986; the second believed in me and imported me to the United States and never stopped supporting me; and the third one selected me for and supported me throughout while on this VP job. To all these people I owe my eternal gratitude.

A big shout out of appreciation to my wife, Celia, my daughters Erika and Renate, my sons-in-law Welbr and David, and my grandchildren Sammy and Elizabeth, for supporting me and allowing me to be five thousand miles away for nearly five years.

To our CEO, who I will personally thank in a few days, I want to mention here my gratitude and appreciation for his time, words of wisdom, and leadership.

To all of you a kiss, a big hug, and abundant peace.

As part of my departure from the church in Brazil, my pastor gave me the opportunity to minister to five hundred leaders of small discipleship groups. I had never seen such a demonstration of affection and outpouring of love toward me as I did at that event. Even though he was only hours away from leaving for Israel, my pastor found the time to take me out for lunch, pray for me, and thank me. I did not understand the reason he was grateful because I did not think I had done anything special for the church, but rather had been blessed there many times.

I landed back in the United States just in time to learn that my daughter Erika was once again expecting, and the boy named Elijah was born in June 2016.

An Invitation and Closing Remarks

I believe that I was brought into this world for a divine purpose, and as long as I live, my job is never complete. There is always someone needing an outstretched arm to pull them up, a shoulder they can lean on, or an ear open and ready to listen. I make a great effort to be a good listener and put the interest of my neighbor ahead of my own.

Many people say that life teaches us invaluable lessons, but indeed it only teaches those willing to learn.

Many people say that life teaches us invaluable lessons, but indeed it only teaches those willing to learn.

I consider myself a winner, but my path to victory was never easy. At every turn, I encountered opposing forces and obstacles I had to overpower. From an organizational standpoint, we all need to report to someone, but that does not mean the person managing you is more intelligent or more capable than you. The fact of the matter is that the incompetent fail on their own. You do not have to focus on exposing them; focus instead on doing your job and doing it well. There are spaces and places for everyone in large organizations.

Since you can reap only what you sow, sow seeds of your own advancement and reap its fruits. If your boss gets in the way and keeps you in the dark, find a place outside of your boss's domain and shine. The world is big enough to have good places and better opportunities for all. When I was asked if I had filled my predecessor's place, my answer was always, "No, I'm in my own place."

The victories that God has allowed me to enjoy and the obstacles that I've conquered have paved the way for my brothers, so that they could leverage my learning for their personal plans for growth and development. Thus God's blessings were not exclusive to me, but have extended to my family and to every person in need of help that God brought my way.

One morning in April 2016, when I was visiting a church in Franklin, Tennessee, the need to buy an area for a charitable organization working in Haiti was discussed. They had been working in recovering and taking care of children living in misery. I paid close attention to the description of the situation of those kids and the atrocities to which some of them had been exposed, and my heart was touched to the point that I made the greatest donation I had ever made. That was possible only because God had blessed me with a heart to do that. I am sure there were people in that service with a much better financial situation than mine. But I do not want to be the one who *has* more—I'd rather be the one who *gives* more. As I wrote earlier in this book, I want people to know my faith through my checkbook and not through my sermons.

I kindly suggest that instead of looking at the size of your problem, you look at the size of the God who can solve it for you. People may attack and think that because they do it behind your back, you will never notice. In fact, we do notice, but because we believe that victory is ahead of us, we do not waste time looking back and paying attention to their sordid attacks. People criticize only those who are defeating them, but because they spend time attacking peers rather than using the same time and energy to engineer their own development, they never move forward. My priority was never to defend myself from attacks, but instead to move ahead so fast that they would not have the strength or speed to reach me.

We all face challenges, and I do not know how to win except by associating with someone who guarantees victories in every battle. As a teenager, I considered myself a self-sufficient person, owner of my decisions and my

I kindly suggest that instead of looking at the size of your problem, you look at the size of the God who can solve it for you.

destiny. One day, however, when I really needed help, I found out that God is the only true expert in every area of life. After drawing close to him, I never again knew defeat. I challenge you to do the same, if you have not yet done so.

As Joshua 1:9 says, "Be strong and courageous. Do not be afraid or terrified because of them, for the Lord your God goes with you; he will never leave you nor forsake you." Life is a one-time and important journey. The way you live it determines your final destination. Do not give command of your ship to anyone who will put you on a collision course or navigate toward failure.

About the Author

Samuel Moody Santos is an engineer, retired Johnson & Johnson vice president of research and development, ordained minister, husband, father, grandfather, former college professor, career coach, and business consultant. He resides in Tennessee and has also worked and lived in Brazil and China. Brazilian born, Samuel is a US citizen with a heart for Jesus Christ and philanthropy.

Printed in the United States
By Bookmasters